"This book [the Secret Teachings of all Ages]
is like unto a door – a gate, in some old sanctuary,
containing within it a wealth of imagery;
a wealth of mysteries, designs and figures."

Manly P. Hall

Unpublished Pages of The Secret Teachings of All Ages

Author: Steven A. Ross

Published by:
Lesscomplicated.net

"This work was reproduced from an original artifact and remains as true to the original as possible. As a reproduction this work contains some errant marks and a few blurred letters. No additional text or comments have been added, by the editor, to the original material."

Published by;

Less Complicated, Inc.
PO BOX 20756
Sedona, AZ 86341

www.lesscomplicated.net

Copyright © 2020 by Steven A. Ross
ISBN: 978-1-7356749-0-2
All rights reserved. No part of the editing or sequencing of special comments may be reproduced or utilized in any form or by any means, electronic or mechanical, including photocopying, recording, or by an information storage and retrieval system, without permission in writing from the editor.

What the World Has Been Missing from Manly P. Hall

"Last Minute Material that Arrived Late to the Printer"

by Steven A. Ross

In the late 1970s, I was encouraged by my colleagues to look more deeply into the writings of Manly P. Hall, Founder and President of the Philosophical Research Society located in Los Feliz, California. Mr. Hall was a highly regarded philosopher, and I had often recognized his name and words featured in various prominent publications.

Since the 1930's, Mr. Hall was known to speak every Sunday morning at the Research Society on a philosophical topic. On Fridays, folks would get together to discuss his points from the previous Sunday's lecture. I decided to visit this group on a Friday afternoon where approximately 60 people had gathered. It was called a Lyceum Meeting. There was a blackboard at the front of the room with approximately seven points listed on the board.

On this special Friday, folks from the Midwest who had listened to Mr. Hall speak since the 1940s were present, all talking together in the front of the room. Most distinctively, there was a woman named Pearl Thomas who was one of the moderators of the meeting. Feeling rather reserved, I nestled my way to the back of the room. In fact, you couldn't get any further than the last row, where I was able to anonymously position myself to listen and observe what was taking place.

Within a few minutes, someone in the audience asked the moderators about one of the points on the blackboard. After a moment of silence, Pearl Thomas called out, "How about you there?" I glanced up, only to see her pointing in my direction. I thought, she couldn't be pointing to me! Yet, as people in the rows before me shifted their positions to the right and the left to clear a space, her gaze was clearly locked on me.

While I can't recall exactly what I said, I responded to her question. Amazingly, heads turned toward me and nodded with smiling faces. When the session was over and I was about to leave, Pearl approached me, asking how long I had been reading the materials of Mr. Hall. I told her I had never read anything he had written. She then asked how many lectures I had attended. I told her I had never before heard Mr. Hall speak. She then informed me she was the head librarian of the Philosophical Research Society Library, and that she would like me to visit her next day. I agreed to do so.

The following day I entered the most magnificent library I had ever seen. It was a two-story chamber, flush with floor to ceiling books, all behind glass. There were paintings, scrolls, busts and numerous, exquisite exhibits. The stately wood bookcases and desks were magnificent beyond words.

A visitor would approach the librarian with a request of a book that they wanted to view, and the librarian would open up the glass case and allow the person to study it on a reading table. Materials dating back to BC were among this rare collection! Incredible parchments and scrolls, paintings and figures were all held in trust here. Undoubtedly, I was viewing one of the greatest collections on earth. I also was told of an inner vault of extremely rare materials that were not made available to the public.

I spoke with Pearl Thomas most of that day as I perused many of the library's holdings.

When I returned the following week, Pearl informed me that whenever I desired to look at one of the books behind the glass cases, I could take the key and open the case myself. What an honor this was for me. I was truly overwhelmed.

Mr. Hall had one of the most outstanding reputations in his field with more books in print than any living author of his time. As I began to familiarize myself with his writings, I found him to be very eclectic, yet he wrote in a manner that was easily understandable, meaning he would write about topics without imposing his own opinion. When he did provide his opinion, he made it quite clear that it was his personal view. It soon became apparent to me that he was more concerned with helping people live fuller and happier lives than writing about topics of phenomena that would awe his readers.

Although in his 70's, Mr. Hall still gave riveting, two-hour lectures for $1. He could speak without notes on any subject. When his lecture materials were eventually typed out, they would generally be 12-15 pages single-spaced. His time was in great demand with so many folks eager to meet with him which made it difficult to arrange a time to meet with him personally.

After three more visits to the Philosophical Research Society (PRS), I had a dream one evening. I perceived that the dream had significance, so I wrote it out and gave it to Pearl Thomas on the following Saturday. Pearl, also in her 70s had listened to Hall speak since she was in her teens, so she knew him very well. She felt that the recounting of my dream should be given to Mr. Hall directly. A week later, I received a call from Mr. Hall himself. He asked me to come visit him in his office.

When I met Mr. Hall, his first words to me were, "Who are you?" I replied that I was a student. He asked me what I wanted from him. I told him that I wanted to go into his vault, review and copy some materials. He then brought up my dream. I told him that it had just come to me. Mr. Hall explained that he had a vision about the PRS nearly six years before he had built it in the 1930s. Yet, he did not build it in the manner he had originally envisioned due to a lack of funds. Even though his earliest vision for the PRS came to him in the 1920s well before I was born in 1949, my dream ironically outlined the details of his original vision.

He gave me permission to go into his inner vault and copy whatever I wished with the agreement that I would not set any of these rare materials into print and sell them as long as he was alive. You see, the reprinting of these old books was the manner by which the PRS was funded. Up until that time, I was the only person who had been allowed to enter Hall's inner vault, remove the holdings and make copies of old manuscripts and books. It was a unique privilege that I hold sacred to this day. With great care, I copied rare writings of the alchemists from the 1500s, 1600s and 1700s along with other, one-of-a-kind manuscripts.

I was led by my spiritual guidance on precisely what to choose, and then spent approximately six months copying those materials from the vault. While I was thrilled to do so, there was one small drawback. Being that the books were so rare and delicate, I couldn't close the top of the copy machine without risking damage to them. Thus, the blinding light of the copier constantly blared into my eyes which affected my eyesight for quite a long time afterward. Perhaps it was a small price to pay for the rare, deeper vision I was given.
One intriguing notebook within the inner vault of Manly P. Hall was titled, "Last Minute Material Arrived Late to the Printer to be Included in the Secret Teachings Book." The date, "1928" was noted on the outside of the book and has never previously appeared.

The following pages herein represent the complete, unedited content that was contained within this notebook, in its original typed version. Mr. Hall explained in a conversation we had together that he had decided to share the abovementioned content in a series of lectures. Only some of the words he shared in his lectures would have appeared within the 'Secret Teachings of All Ages' book, yet this lecture series allowed Mr. Hall to expand on the content he wished to include. They were dated in 1928—the same year that the original printing of the Secret Teachings book was initially published.

I would like to share the following words of the "last minute material" by Mr. Hall right here in this intro so you can have a fuller understanding of this brilliant man's intent. These words appear later within this book in the sections when and where he actually expressed them. Here is what Manly P. Hall said.

"When you start reading the book [Secret Teachings], we do not want you to approach it with any illusions—any misconceptions of its contents. It is called an Encyclopedia; it is an Encyclopedia of symbols. More than simply symbols, it is an effort to begin an interpretation of these symbols. It is not intended to be a creation that claims any merit from the standpoint that it is new or unusual."

"The book is not esoteric; it is simply a reconstruction of the gateways of ancient learning; it is the Front Door—nothing more. It does not tell you very much; it is simply that path leading up to ancient wisdom. You will find in it 45 chapters—all presumably different—and yet all exactly the same; it may be some time before you notice the repetitions; 45 chapters tell one story and repeat it again and again and again. But each chapter repeats it in a different way—reaching a different type of mind. The book is simply a guide in direction; a book on the subject of these teachings cannot, and never has, and never will, reveal the teaching; but if you are willing to take it and work with it conscientiously, we believe you will derive from it material which will help you to reconstruct what is not there—to see what is not written—to discover what is not on the page itself."

"We have spent a great deal of time in the archives of ancient philosophy trying to discover the order and sequence of these different mysteries; we have found on every hand one cry going up: 'This is a most interesting subject but unfortunately there isn't anything known about it— there is no information available.' We have worked very hard to find the scraps that could be discovered and have sought to place them together according to their own nature; therefore do not be surprised if you find apparent contradictions on every page—there is no effort made to make the different systems conform—it is more valuable that they be as they are. The information is presented, as far as possible, in the spirit of the original writing. It is not what you are going to get by reading this book that will help you; it is what you will get if you will think about what you read. Read it alone—by yourself; the first step to knowing is independence."

"We believe the pointers in this book will assist you to reconstruct the body of world learning; it is only the individual who does the work that gets ahead—the power to do things. This is the very kernel –the basis of philosophy, because philosophy is simply knowledge, and knowledge comes from a certain activity that is necessary in order to understand."

"Accident and design have conspired to delay this book, and to make it as difficult as possible. This book is built and prepared— as far as we could do it—in the same style that the ancients gave their knowledge to the world; it is built and presented in a style appropriate to the subject matter; it is as beautiful as the printer's craft could make it; everything that goes into the making of it is as beautiful as could be secured; we have verified, checked and rechecked everything in the book; the material is literally true. The important thing will be to reconstruct out of the book one thought; it is written around one thought—and the discovery of that one thought is the supreme achievement in reading the book. The material there represents one end of an endless thread that winds out in all parts of creation –as long as space is broad, and as deep as the profundities of the Abyss."

"This book is like unto a door— a gate, in some old sanctuary, containing within it a wealth of imagery; a wealth of mysteries, designs and figures. When you have wandered therein you might say to yourself; 'I wish I had a guide to tell me what these things mean.' And you will find your guide to be your own rational soul." **-- Manly P. Hall - 1928.**

These words from Manly Hall are deep and profound yet I have never read them in any publication attached to the Secret Teachings book. It has now been over 40 years since I was in Manly Hall's personal vault. Since these words have never before been published, and since I promised Mr. Hall that I would not make public any of the materials he entrusted to me until after his death, I now feel compelled to make this information available to his many followers around the world.

Manly Hall's body of work has had a profound impact upon my life, and I am confident this additional content, originally intended to be part of his most acclaimed book of all times, can have a positive impact upon yours.

With all best wishes on your journey,

Steven A. Ross
Date 8/20/2020

Table of Contents

Introductory Meeting .... pg. 13

Lectures

1. Agents and Elements Used to Perpetuate Knowledge .... pg. 19
2. Major Constitution of the Line .... pg. 25
3. The Constitution of the Circle .... pg. 31
4. Potentialities and Potencies .... pg. 35
5. Differences Between Knowledge and Belief .... pg. 39
6. The Discipline of Facts .... pg. 43
7. Observation – Discrimination - Concentration .... pg. 47
8. Relationship of Symbolism to the Human Body .... pg. 51
9. Relationship of Symbolism to Man II .... pg. 55
10. Relationship of Symbolism to Man III .... pg. 59
11. Symbolism and Ritualism .... pg. 65
12. Symbolism (cont'd) - Neo Platonism .... pg. 69
13. Symbolism (cont'd) – The Quaternary .... pg. 75
14. Relationship Existing Between Substance of Mind and Spirit .... pg. 79
15. Esotericism and Exotericism .... pg. 83
16. Numbers .... pg. 87
17. The Bembine Table of Isis .... pg. 91
18. On Use of the Book – Bibliography and the Index .... pg. 97
19. Symbolism .... pg. 101
20. Consciousness-Mental Level-Materialism (Concerning the Book) .... pg. 105

1) Introductory Meeting......................... May 28, 1928
2) Agents and Elements Used to Perpetuate
     Knowledge .... May 29, 1928
3) Major Constitution of the Line, The;
     Coming Out of the Dot............ May 30, 1928
     (Savior Gods of the Ages)
4) The Constitution of the Circle...... May 31, 1928
5) Potentialities and Potencies .... June 1, 1928
6) Differences Between Knowledge and
     Belief .... June 2, 1928
7) The Discipline of Facts .... June 3, 1928
8) Observation - Discrimination - Con-
     centration .... June 4, 1928
9) Relationship of Symbolism to the
     Human Body .... June 5, 1928
10) Relationship of Symbolism to Man (II)   June 6, 1928
11) Relationship of Symbolism to Man (III) June 8, 1928
12) Symbolism and Ritualism .... June 9, 1928
13) Symbolism (cont'd.)-Neo-Platonism .. June 10, 1928

14) Symbolism (cont'd.)- The Quaternary.... June 11, 1928
15) Relationship Existing Between Substance
      of Mind and Substance of Spirit ...... June 12, 1928
16) Esotericism and Exotericism .... June 13, 1928
17) Numbers .... June 14, 1928
18) The Bembine Table of Isis .... June 15, 1928
19) On Use of the Book - Bibliography and
      the Index .... June 16, 1928
20) Symbolism .... June 17, 1928
21) Consciousness-Mental Level-Materialism
      (Concerning the Book) .... June 18, 1928

INTRODUCTORY MEETING FOR THE MATERIALS THAT ARRIVED TOO LATE TO BE INCLUDED IN "THE SECRET TEACHINGS"

Manly P. Hall   5/28/1928

Unpublished Pages of "*The Secret Teachings of All Ages*"

LECTURES BY MANLY P. HALL

San Francisco, California

May 28th to June 18, 1928.

INTRODUCTORY MEETING

These talks are designed primarily to serve you in two ways: First, to give you further commentary material on the subject of the book; Second - that I may bring to you the last-minute material I could not get in the book.

The most perfect, the most profound symbol in the Universe is the blank piece of paper. The blank piece of paper, in symbolism, is the proper emblem of complete power; in other words, the blank paper is the symbol of 'Absolute Life'. The moment you put anything on that paper you limit Life. You do something to destroy the perfection of it; consequently this blank piece of paper is the emblem of the Absolute. Every figure and symbol that you draw is drawn on the paper - therefore, it is the symbol of the conditions that Space is capable of producing. The paper - blank - is the ALL; and everything you draw upon it is some Part of All. But the moment you draw anything on it the All is lost, and some part comes into being.

In symbolism we are working with universal forces and agents; every one of these forces or agents is an expression of Space. Why? Because Space is the ultimate of substance - the ultimate of force - the ultimate of intelligence - and the sum of them all. Nothing exists except that it exists in Space. Nothing is made, but that it is made of Space; Space is the absolute origin of everything. Space is the absolute substance from which all things are fashioned. In Egypt it is called 'THAT'. The paper represents the perfect origin of everything; it is not God; it is not Man; it is not the Universe; it is supreme and superior to them all.

What Space represents in its abstract and absolute sense we find in every activity of Nature; Space and absolute Spirit are one; Space and absolute Matter are one; therefore, Space, Spirit and Matter are one. Spirit is the positive manifestation of Space; Matter is the negative manifestation of Space; Spirit and Matter exist together in Space; Space, Spirit and Matter are the first Trinity, with Space the Father, Spirit the Son, and Matter, the Holy Ghost.

To return to our piece of paper: the most primitive emblem is the Dot. What does the Dot signify? It simply represents the All, considered as The One. Man, attempting to understand the Absolute, cannot do it. Therefore he concentrates the Absolute mentally into a point - a focal point - and he has the Dot. The Dot is the first illusion. The reason why the Dot is the first illusion is because it is the first departure from things as they eternally are. There is nothing immortal ultimately but Space; there is nothing eternal, but Space; there is nothing that has neither beginning nor end but Space; there is nothing that is unchangeable, but Space. Everything that grows grows out of Space; Space remains.

Mentally and philosophically, Space is synonomous with Self. The Self is as abstruse, as abstract, as the blank piece of paper. If man can find the nature of the blank piece of paper he can find himself. The Dot, in the middle of the paper, is what we call the Spirit; the Spirit is Self - with the loss of something - the loss of limitlessness. The Dot is the first limitation of the Self; the Dot is the first limitation of Space, and Spirit is the first limitation of Self.

The blank paper is Life, every where and unlimited; the Dot is Life, as a center. According to the law of Being, the Dot must some time be erased, because nothing but the blank paper is eternal in Philosophy. The Dot represents a limitation; the life that is everywhere becomes the life that is somewhere. The Life which is All Life becomes the life limited; the Dot is the first separation; the first limitation; it is the first time that the All ceases to be All, and becomes One.

When there is no Dot there is nothing to take away; that which remains cannot die; it cannot be added to or taken from, but the moment you put the Dot on the paper you can take your pencil and rub it out, and then you have the white paper again, because the white paper is emblematic of Eternity, and the Dot is Time. The Time is dissolved in Eternity. We trace our origin from the Dot, which is the primitive seed; the egg- laid in Space. The Dot is the first impermanent thing. When we view existence from the Self downward into the illusion, the Dot is the first degree of illusion. The least degree of impermanence is the greatest degree of permanence. That which comes the nearest to being divine is the least degree limited by mortal things; in other words, good is the least degree of evil, and evil the least degree of good. The Dot being nearest to perfection of all symbols, is the least imperfect of all symbols. It comes closes to being All. The Dot is called the Sacred Island; it is the beginning of existence, the beginning of mortal life, whether it is the life of man or universe. It is the germ - that which is limitless, in existence is manifesting in a limited way in the Dot. The Dot manifests in an active way; it appears on the fields of Space; but Space is forever.

When we consider ourselves we always think of our spirit as the greatest thing in us and of us. Our spirit is our real self - we feel that. Our spirit is the germ, bursting forth like a seed - becomes all that we are. We understand, for a moment, the teachings of the Brahman and the Vedantist; for Nirvana, in the abstract sense, means the reabsorption into the Eternal Self. (Attaining absolute immortality).

The most primitive forms in the universe are the Dot, the Line and the Circle. These are the supreme symbols. The Dot is the spirit, and the Spirit is 'I'. The 'I' in its original form in Hebrew - the yad - represents the seed. Let us imagine, for a moment, that we are going to project the 'I' into manifestation; the 'I' is Itself - and Itself alone.

There are three ways by which we can know anything:
(1) By analysis of its own inherent nature.
(2) Through comprehension of its activity or manifestation (we know what a thing is by learning what it does)
(3) By knowing the Effect of what it does upon something else. (Prof. James' theory of Pragmatism).

* * * * * * *

The Dot is the 'I', or the germ of existence.
The Line is the dot, elongated; strings of dots - because the one line is simply made up of little germ lives (Monadic lives of Leibnitz). A line is therefore the symbol of the Dot, moving; it is the activity of the dots. Our key thought is, therefore, the Line is the MOTION of the Dot. There is only one way in which a Dot can move; and that is - away from itself; therefore, all motion is away from Self. In the process of creation all motion is away from Self. In the process of return again, from creation to the primeval or first state, all motion is toward Self. Involution is motion away from; Evolution is motion towards - Self.

The Self is the Dot; the Self, moving away from itself, projects the Line; which becomes the radius of an imaginary circle, which is the power of that central Dot. Every human mind has a place beyond which it cannot think; there is a limit to our 'awareness'. The Circle is the symbol of all limits; it is the symbol of the end of things. Therefore we have the Dot, the Line and the Circle - the three perfect symbols - the first symbols known to man - the Cause, the Action, and the Effect. In these three simple emblems you have the key to all knowledge; there is no knowledge that is not in the Dot, the Line and the Circle - but only the Master can extract it all. The Dot is Consciousness; the Line is Intelligence, and the Circle is Force.

In Man the Dot is Spirit; the Line is conscious activity or intelligence; the Circle is the Body. The Body is the limit of the radius of activity of Mind. The Dot is Truth, or Reality - whatever form it may take; the Line is activity; the Circle is the symbol of the Effect of that activity. The blade of grass is but a symbol of a degree of consciousness; Man is a symbol of a degree of consciousness; it is the effect of a certain rate of consciousness working on substance. Consciousness acting upon matter creates Form. Matter is not form; matter, like Space, is spread all over everywhere. The activity of life upon it 'curdles' it and it forms bodies. Therefore, the form, which is the body which we recognize, is simply the result of a rate of life working on matter and moulding it into an organism. It is held together by the conscious agent working in it; the moment this agent is removed from it, the process of returning to simple primordial conditions takes place.

* * * * * *

The Dot is the symbol of Philosophy, because Philosophy is the least degree of illusion that exists; we do not say it is Truth - but the least degree of illusion. Philosophy is relatively the nearest thing we have to Truth, therefore it is as close to Truth as anything can be. It is as close to the Absolute as the most primitive form can be; the Dot, being the simplest thing we can put on the paper, is nearest to perfection - Truth. Philosophy is to the white paper - Absolute Truth - what your Dot is to Reality. Philosophy is capable of telling man the nature or substance of the white paper. The Dot will never know the substance of the paper; nor will Philosophy know the absolute substance of reality. Philosophy is an immovable thing; the moment motion is added you cease to have philosophy and you have Theology; it is a gesture; it is the Dot, walking out of itself. The Line of Theology is shown by its nature; it is not a fixed element, as is philosophy, but subject to vicissitudes - is emotional, changeable and violent. Theology is properly symbolized by the Line.

The Line is the radius of an imaginary circle; Science is the circle. Science is the limitation of the outpouring manifestation. Science represents the physical body of knowledge; the mental or spiritual body of knowledge is philosophy; therefore man ascends from Science, through Theology, to Philosophy.

We have another group we must consider: the Dot is the proper symbol of Cause; the Cause of things. The Circle is the proper symbol of the Effect. The Line, that unites them, is the symbol of the activity which causes the Cause to manifest into an Effect.

In these primitive symbols we have the elements of the world; the Dot is Heaven; the Line, Earth; and the Circle, Hell - the three worlds of Christian Theology. Heaven is the spiritual nature of God; Earth is the material nature of God; Hell is the place where God ceases to be - the outer circumference, where the light fails - and technically it represents in our system of thinking the physical universe, because here the life God is the weakest. Physical life is the point where spiritual life leaves off.

Spirit is only one-fifth as active in the physical world as it is in the spiritual world. The reason we have a physical world is because we have only one-fifth the activity here we have in our higher natures; this makes this the material universe. The material universe is the circumference; the divine world is the center.

THE THREE WORLDS

HEAVEN
(God the Father)

EARTH
(God, the Son)

HELL
(God the Holy Spirit)
(Jehovah)
(Shiva)
(Osiris)

Zeus / Jupiter
Neptune
Pluton

1 o
2
3
4
5
6
The Physical Sun (Dot) 7
The Vital Ethers (Line) 8
Physical Matter (Circle) 9

(9 Mos of Prenatal Man)

* * * * * *

In Grammar: the noun is the Dot; the verb, the Line; the object, the circumference.
You will find the same thing in musical tones; in color - always the trinity of the Dot, the Line and the Circle. You can dream on and around these for the rest of life; for it is always the triangle - the proper emblems of the universe. It is necessary to build upon these diagrammatic principles; the three worlds are the Supreme, the Superior, and the Inferior worlds of Plato.

Whosoever sees the Son, sees the Father.
The Path of the soul to the Dot is
through the line, the bridge connecting
Cause and Effect.

* * * * * * *

Lecture # 1

AGENTS AND ELEMENTS USED TO PERPETUATE KNOWLEDGE

Manly P. Hall   5/29/1928

Unpublished Pages of "*The Secret Teachings of All Ages*"

LECTURES BY MANLY P. HALL

NO. 1
5/29/28

AGENTS AND ELEMENTS USED TO PERPETUATE KNOWLEDGE

The blank piece of paper is the only answer to the problem of absolute knowledge. Absolute knowledge is only to be symbolized by the blank, untouched, unconditioned sheet of paper.

Try to remember the work of last evening, and from that point we will continue to develop the theory of knowledge. The first question that must arise is: what is knowable? The question is not: 'what can we know in our present condition'. The question is: 'what is knowable'? The answer to that question can only be determined by a consideration of the methods and processes and mechanism of knowledge. Let us remember our Dot, our Line and Circle; for they are the only three methods whereby we can know anything or learn anything about it. The first is by a study or consideration of the nature of a thing, as it is. The second is by a consideration and study of the activity or life principle innate in a thing. And the third method of knowing is by an analysis or consideration of the effect produced by the activity of a thing. Therefore we study it according to its own nature, according to its own action, and according to the effects of its own action. We have therefore three ways of knowing; of finding out the nature of a certain desired object.

If we study an object from a consideration of the effect which is produced, we are then largely concerned with the utilitarian nature of the object itself; its use, and the thing which it produces or does - the effect; and we accept or reject things according to the effects they produce. Science is largely concerned with the study of the effects - of the activity of things. Of what things are - science has no knowledge. If you will study the system by which we secure words and names you will find nearly all the things are called by a name that is equivalent to their effect. That was the primary idea.

Physically we can never study the Cause of anything; we might modify that, and say there are a few things we can study the approximate cause; we can see the effects; the principle of a living thing can never be known by physical sense perceptions. To know a thing really, we must study its own nature; this we cannot do at the present time. Physically our knowledge is limited to the classification of the known effects and agencies. Now mentally, we can transcend effects, and enter into the sphere of processes. Science works with the circumference; philosophy dares to work with the Line. Philosophy dares to investigate the cause behind the effect; therefore philosophy may be likened to that faculty or power in nature which attempts to unite the cause and its effect by describing the activity which, radiating from the cause, produces the effect. Therefore, Cause still remains unknown. But those who are capable of studying the radiant energy which, coming from the cause produces effects, are closer to the cause than those studying the effect itself. Philosophy then is higher than science; it deals with the element closer to cause than science can deal with.

The part with which we are particularly concerned in all study, and in all questing for knowledge, is that part which links the cause and its effect. We are not yet equipped with a conscious mechanism sufficiently accurate to investigate cause. We cannot know a thing as it is, but we can come closer to the knowledge of things as they are by considering the effect of things, and the vast mechanism of sidereal law, by which the universe is controlled, is discovered through the disciplines of philosophy. Philosophy is either one of two forms; absolute philosophy and relative philosophy. Absolute philosophy is something which relative philosophy postulates. For example: we are all trying to be good; and by that act we create an image of perfect goodness. We all believe there is some where, some time, a perfect condition of the thing we are functioning with, in part. Philosophy says there is absolute knowledge some where, and we will reach it if we try hard enough, and long enough. That is - some philosophers say that.

Mankind ponders, but he knows nothing. In philosophy, absolute knowledge is the perfect thing hoped for; and relative knowledge is the thing we have at hand to work with. All knowledge belonging to man is relative, because it depends upon a partly evolved nature; consequently the unfinished mind is incapable of producing a finished product. We have relative knowledge in the world, and absolute knowledge as an ideal aspired to.

Let us return again to the subject of our blank sheet of paper; it is symbolic of absolute knowing because being the symbol of everything, it is the absolute state of everything. The absolute is a very exalted state; in fact, it is the ultimate. We can intelligently conceive it; to make an effort to tell what that ultimate is, is fatal. The absolute is the vanishing point of our own comprehension; we cannot conceive of anything beyond it. Tomorrow our comprehension is bigger - we know more; but the absolute is still just as far away.

Philosophy knows certain things; the first thing is the nature of knowledge, in its relative sense. Relative knowledge embraces everything that you put on the blank sheet of paper. Absolute knowledge is the subject of the paper itself. Our work on this subject describes the blank sheet of paper in the only way it can be described - not by telling what it is, but by telling what it is not. We eliminate the conceivable, and that which is left is the inconceivable; therefore the absolute represents that which is left - when everything you can think of is gone.

****

This evening we are to consider the dawn of philosophy - the history of human reason. Working outward from the Unknown - we cannot work with absolute powers, so we begin - not with Space, but with God, the Dot, or the beginning of things. What is God? God is best defined as: "A first manifestation of infinite existence". God must always be like us - what we are - the makers of It. We have the First Manifestation of absolute life; what it is we do not know, but we have made it something; It remains; the highest form we can attribute to it is the highest form we know; and that is the sphere - the most perfect known form - consequently it is used as a symbol of the Deity. It remains simply the first manifestation of unmanifested Power. As we go higher in our knowledge, this God becomes more magnificent to us; we begin to understand the fact that all of the powers of Infinite Being flow into creation through its central point - the beginning of thing. The least material, and most spiritual, of created creatures. Older than anything coming from it, yet younger than the youngest thing that comes from it. Therefore God in the greatest and most universal sense is the Point established in the Absolute, through which it manifests forth into tangible existence; it is The All made One. Deity has had many attributes, many conditions; the description of Plato is that: 'Deity is the Self-moving, Unmoved, All-moving Source.'

Now comes the question: if the absolute is unlimited and unconditioned, why and how do these Points (imperfect things) come out of the Perfect Thing? The reason for that is perhaps one of the most daring of postulates. (The nature of your search is knowledge; in the beginning you do not know; you begin by wanting to know, and you keep on until you find out.)

When it comes to considering an abstract form as great as the law controlling the absolute, we have nothing but hypothesis. It is the supreme hypothesis; that is, the nature and substance of universal law. We assume this point. (Analogy is man's greatest tool - Hermes). He has applied it to every condition of human existence; he projects it into the unknown. Let us, therefore, use a simple analogy. When you are asleep you are, to a degree, resembling Illusion. The state of sleep is the nearest thing we have to the piece of paper; you do not know you are; you have no sense of time, place, etc. The state of sleep is the 'Little Death' - sleep and death are the twin sisters. Sleep is related to the state of the Absolute. When you go to sleep you forget the world; but you do not forget certain things; if you have always arisen at 6:30 - you will sleep and have no knowledge, but at 6:30 you awake. What is the thing that makes you do that? The answer is 'Habit'. And you discover this condition of comparative unconsciousness is subject to habit, and although you know nothing about it, your habit is stronger than your unawareness. What are the forces that are moving the Universe? What are the agents and elements that control the absolutely blank piece of paper? And cause it to periodically spawn forth worlds, and draw them in again? The most daring conclusion of the ages is 'Habit'. Habit is something stronger than the sleeping consciousness of an individual; it is something that awakens the sleeper when he cannot awake himself; therefore, the coming and going of creations upon the face of infinite existence are the results of a law, and that law is Periodicity - the law of Habit of Infinite Space. It is the supreme habit of the absolute; t is the habit of Eternity to create and to dissolve.

Periodically on the face of All Being there appear the centers of life; the germs, the seeds of worlds. The first seed, the embryo of Creation, as a whole, is called God - in the highest sense of that term. It is the First Thing to awake; it is the highest degree of consciousness. It is older than any of the parts of itself; the One that controls all parts is greater than the parts; God is The One - the Seed that appears, waking and sleeping, periodically in Duration. The Dot is the symbol of Deity in toto - in itself. "The Universe is made up of Monads, all enclosed in one great Germ." (Leibnitz).

From the sheet of paper we have moved to the Dot. In the Dot we have Deity. It is our opinion that man's whole evolution - all that he hopes to be - depends on his concept of God. Why? Because his concept of God is a thermometer under his tongue; it tells what he is. No nation or race can be greater than its concept of God. His concepts of God pass through three states; God is either a Personality (the circumference), an Individuality (the Line) or a Spirituality (the Dot), or an Actuality (the blank paper). The day of worshipping personal gods is dying out; we are now considering Deity as a cosmic principle of Reality, radiating through all the Universe - an immense Power, and we are beginning to realize that we understand less and less about this Power. We are beginning to realize the immensity of this Deity; God is growing: God has always been the same - but man's idea of God changes and assumes loftier proportion.

In manifestation, form is the least permanent of all conditions of space; consequently he who takes his stand upon a rock will have it crumble; he who stands on space will never lose it. Plato divides all manifestation into certain divisions; the Dot ght be termed the heart of existence; all existence depends on that first germ for all that it is; it is called the foundation of the universe. The Law of Relative Importance. First of all, if you have a number of things depending upon each other, that which is fundamental among those dependencies is first. For example: you are on a ship, and the ship carries a number of thing. If you throw a box overboard the ship will go on; but if you sink the ship, the box will go down with it. The ship does not depend on the box. If you destroy that which is fundamental you tear down everything with it. You come to the conclusion, in philosophy, that things are greater or lesser according to the things they depend on, and the things that depend on them. Man is master over the things that depend on him, and is mastered by everything he depends on. Gods are greater than men because men depend on them; they represent the principles of existence. upon which all creatures depend. Remove the principle, and all men die; therefore every creature is judged according to the relationship he occupies to his dependencies and to the things he depends upon.

****

What is the most important thing in the universe? 'Understanding' is the one answer. There is nothing greater. Everything depends on that. It is the sum of knowledge; the sum of Wisdom; the sum of thinking; the sum of dreaming. It is not intellectualism; it is understanding; and understanding is the realization of things. That which we understand, we do. We have known about Christ for 2000 years, but we have not done anything; because we have never realized what It is. To understand is the ultimate condition of knowledge; it is the perfect realization of the purpose and meaning of things - and he who possesses it lives well.

****

Lecture # 2

MAJOR CONSTITUTION OF THE LINE; THE COMING OUT OF THE DOT AND SAVIOR GODS OF THE AGES

Manly P. Hall   5/30/1928

Unpublished Pages of "*The Secret Teachings of All Ages*"

LECTURES BY MANLY P. HALL   NO. 2
                                                                      5/30/28.

THE MAJOR CONSTITUTION OF THE LINE, COMING OUT OF THE DOT

(Savior Gods of the Ages)

****

Light is an appropriate symbol of Life; the nature of Light is to radiate. Light is radiant; and having considered the source of Life, we will now consider the radiance or outpouring from life. This outpouring is summed up in symbolism in a simple verticle line, drawn from above downward. The Dot may be likened to the flame of a candle; and an analysis of the flame reveals that it is in three parts; namely, the three phases of the Dot. The blue is the heart of the candle flame; the folden radiance that surrounds it; and the reddish flame at the circumference; this is the three-fold nature of the candle flame; this is the nature of Fire. Because of its nature - its triune nature - Fire is used to symbolize God; and the worship of fire is an ancient institution.

From the flame itself outward there continually pours a radiance, illuminating that which is about the central flame. This radiance is most like the flame where it touches the flame, and least like the flame at the outer circumference, or area of its light. Light is simply a rate of vibration; it pours outward from a center of a vibratory ray. For the sake of the symbolism, we relate the flame to the Dot, the radiance pouring outward to the Line, and the wall where darkness absorbs the light is the circle.

This evening we are to presume the nature of the Dot is comprehended; therefore we will now analyze the relationship of the ray to its source.

Think a moment of your candle flame; the heart of the flame is colorless; where the light is least you have the heart of the flame; In philosophy the Dot is invisible, intangible, and incapable of being analyzed. But the radiance coming from it is light; mental light, physical and spiritual light. The activity of this radiance is capable of analysis. The Dot is, therefore, called the Hidden Father; the Light, the Brilliant Son, born out of the Father, and representing the Father before Creation.

Now let us analyze, physically, the constitution of radiance. What is this intangible something that is continually pouring off from centers of life, and is termed 'activity'? Radiance is a Motion; a condition and a state. Radiance is the continual effort of central forces to expand; we know that in the universe there is a continual activity; this activity is two-fold. First, an effort of all life to expand; second - an effort of all substance to resist expansion. Therefore in form we have a continual expansion from within, and a pressure from without to balance it. Every organism is so composed in nature to fit the pressure which closes in around it. The moment man leaves the surface of the earth he must readjust himself, because the pressure upon him changes; therefore, environment is a form of pressure. The more material the environment, the greater the pressure - consequently the greater the difficulty to expand. The higher the environment the less pressure thereis; until pressure reaches a vanishing point. There being nothing pressing upon the nature of a body, consciousness is diffused through all things.

What is growth? Growth is a struggle of life to control its environment. It is evident that the more we find what substance is, the more easily it is influenced. It is easier to control a highly organized vehicle than a vehicle of lower organization. Perfect liberty, perfect freedom, is the goal of living. All things are continually struggling to be free, and freedom lies in perfect manifestation. There is but one freedom - perfection. Freedom consists in becoming master of environment; it is not necessarily a physical thing; it usually is not. Every creature is a slave to those parts of itself which are not responding to the impulses of its internal life. Every individual is therefore a slave to his own material constitution; he is a prisoner held in by the walls of unresponsive substance; therefore the natural process of existence is an effort to control environment and to make it responsive. This is the symbolism of the Line. The line is a potential cosmic nerve-ray which gives sensibility, and consciousness. Man controls his physical body by ever increasing the acuteness of his nerve functions. The nerve is simply an impulse-carrier, that is giving more consciousness over parts of what was previously an unconscious and non-responsive substance. Nerves are becoming ever more acute in their function; they are bringing man more knowledge concerning the nature of the substance which composes his world.

****

A few special definitions:

The Line is the outpouring of Cause into Effect. It is life's effort to permeate its environment with the qualities of the first innate life principle. It is the effort of the center to make the circumference like itself.

The reason for growth is simply that life, innately perfect, gradually shall objectify its perfection. In other words, the potentialities of life gradually become objective potencies or powers, and growth is bringing the inside of life to the outside. It is the motion from within - outward. It is the effort of life to unite its conscious qualities to its environment; this is expansion, and life is not a ray going in any particular direction; but it is an expansion.

Not only is life an expansion from within outward; but it is an unfoldment of potential powers. Growth has, as its ultimate goal, the bringing into conscious expression all the seed germs of power lying latent within every germ of existence. Man, the Dot - the germ - contains within it all potentialities; the purpose of this growth is an effort to escape imprisonment. Form is a prison; tje more life expresses itself the less of a prison form is.

We are a threefold creation. Plato established a triangle as the three parts making up any problem. The triangle in man is his spirit, his body and the link that connects them. In the universe it is the Divine creation, the elemental creation, and the link that connects them. The divine universe, composed of divine energy, and the material universe, composed of material energy, may be likened to the spiritual nature in man and to the body of man. Assuming the spirit to be the controlling part of man, and the body the controlled part - the spirit could not control the body were it not for connecting links which unite the two bodies.

Abstract truth, as a divine element, on one hand; and physical material mankind, as an ignorant element, on the other; here we have Reality - and here we have Man, who needs reality. Reality is the life principle; man is the material being. Mankind, in its ignorant state, and absolute truth, in its perfect state - are the two opposites of the universe. Truth knows no man; man knows no truth. One a measureless boundless reality; the other - Man - who does not recognise knowledge. Reality is the Dot; mankind the circle. You have to have the line to join the two together - a mediator. God is the proper emblem of Truth and Life; Matter is the emblem of ignorance, error, death.

Neither of them can blend, in their absolute state. How are you going to get them together? That is the problem of the Line. It is the reconciling principle that must always exist.

Facts are divine principles. Between every fact and man there stands some sort of a mediator, some instructor. Between knowledge, and the one who desires to know stands a personality, in the physical world, who possesses the knowledge and is capable of imparting it to another. Everywhere in nature there is a mediating principle that communicates the knowledge of one thing to another thing desiring the knowledge. It must necessarily be in contact with both extremes at the same time; must have the ability to contact both extremes. The mediator must be able to ascend to the higher, and descend to the lower.

According to philosophy there are three kinds of creaturs; Gods, who know; men do not know; and God-Men or Men-Gods, who act as the mediator between the two. (Pythagoras).

GOD THE FATHER	○	THE KNOWER: The Sphere of Reality Dwelling Place of the Gods
GOD THE SON	○	Composed of 2 kinds of Beings; Demigods that come down from the 1st into the first half of the 2nd World; From Below up come the Supermen, and these two meet.
GOD THE HOLY SPIRIT	○	The Sphere of Ignorance; occupied by inferior beings, including Man and all elemental creatures in whom the state of knowing is unawakened.

In the second sphere we have two kinds of creatures; those who are divine but partake somewhat of the material creation - the demigods. And those coming up from below Supermen, but who are not gods - although more than men. Here the more-than-Men blend with the less-than-Gods; consequently it may be said that the instructors of humanity are of two kinds; demigods and supermen. The Demigods represent the conditions of knowledge that can never come down to matter, but come part way down; and the Supermen represent that knowledge that ascends out of ignorance to a state of partial knowing. The knowledge of the gods partakes of the perfect knowledge and is backed by the consciousness of Causes; the knowledge of the Supermen represents that which can be given by a human being, aspiring to perfect knowledge but not yet finding it; therefore it does not partake of Cause.

According to Plato, the Demigods can never be men; they are not human but they can come down, in consciousness, low enough to reach the highest point human consciousness can reach. Therefore they can blend. Supermen are conditions of knowing which have increased from human knowing to a point proximate to divine knowing. (Socrates' daemon; Pythagoras overshadowed by the spirit of the Pythian Apollo) According to philosophy, the overshadowing Deity is the Demigod, or the rate of knowing which has its source in Absolute Truth. Whereas the Man was the Superman who had raised himself to the point where he could contact the Demigods, who descended from the heavens. (Jesus, the Man; Christos, the Demigod). The World Savior is the Superman, en rapport with the Demigod. In Him the link between the cause and the effect is established. From above he receives Life, and from

NO. 3
5/31/28

below he gives it to the world. Being a man, he is still one with man and can reach him; but he is capable of receiving from above, and giving to the below. The Theory of Polarity; the Above and the Below united.

What, then, is the purpose of Philosophy?

To raise every man to the level of that spiritual state, wherein being lifted as high as man can lift him, he can reach the lowest rung of the celestial ladder. He who becomes elevated becomes a Superman.

****

The Dot, in the center of the Circle, is the Rational Soul.
The Irrational Soul is that part of man's nature that does not know Self. The qualities of the rational soul are understanding, realization, comprehension. (Unselfishness) The qualities of the irrational soul are ignorance, lust (Selfishness). The rational soul is the conscious part of the Universe (the Dot); the irrational soul is the unconscious part of the Universe (Circle). Socrates defines Man: 'The Self-knowing Being immersed in a not-knowing body'. The philosophic resurrection is the resurrection of the rational soul out of the sepulchre of the irrational nature; the Line is the redeemer, through whom all things are eventually lifted up to light.

The acme of human knowing is the Superman, who, having reached this state, comes to the point where he is capable of cognizing the consciousness of the divine sphere. The dwelling place of the Superman and the dwelling place of the Demigod is called the Sphere of Light.

(3 Worlds: (1) Life
             (2) Light
             (3) Heat)

****

Lecture # 3

THE CONSTITUTION OF THE CIRCLE

Manly P. Hall   5/31/1928

Unpublished Pages of "*The Secret Teachings of All Ages*"

LECTURES BY MANLY P. HALL   NO. 3

5/31/28

THE CONSTITUTION OF THE CIRCLE

The One is before Being, because Being is a condition of The One, and consequently dependent upon it. The Dot is One, in Platonic and Pythagorean philosophy. The Line is The Beautiful; the Circle is The Good. This is the Platonic Triad - The One, The Beautiful, The Good.

The One is before all Numbers; it is called the capstone of the pyramid of Numbers. All numbers are simply aggregations of 'One'. Two is two ones. The power of One is stability; the staying-power - permanence. The One is the Eternal Permanent; The Beautiful is the Eternal Flow (Beauty, in philosophy, is akin to Motion); Beauty is active - the flow of the One. The Good, which is the third, and the least power, is that which contains or accepts into itself the nature of the Beautiful. He who contains the Beautiful is The Good, for goodness is the result of the manifestation of innate Beauty; that which has in its soul Beauty, radiates Good.

From this Platonic definition you will realize why the Savior Gods of all nations have been symbolized as Beautiful. In Ethics, beauty is the redeeming power; when the human soul opens itself to the reception of beauty, it is then transmuted. Plotinus gives us the secret of the entire philosophy: 'Beauty is a force; it is a radiant power, and no one can come into the presence of it and remain unmoved'. Beauty is an internal force, manifesting through Good, and Good - in its last analysis - is simply the symmetrical and harmonious coadunation of parts. That is good in which the parts work together; that individual is good in whom all natural forces are functioning naturally.

Our prime consideration this evening is to consider the philosophy of the nature of the Circle as used in Symbolism. The circle is the circumference of the radius. We must concern ourselves with the nature of the circumference of Being. In harmony with our previous work, showing the outpouring of life from the center to the circumference, we find the circle to represent the outer extremity of the area of consciousness - awareness. The circle corresponds to the inferior nature of everything; the Dot the Superior nature; the Line, the mediating nature. The inferior nature of the mind is the concrete or animal mentality; the superior nature of the mind is the conscious or spiritual intellection - the cognating principle. The superior part of the mind is the rational mind; the superior part of the soul is the rational soul. The superior part of the body (physical body of man) is consciousness; the inferior part is Form. Between all of these bodies there are mediating principles.

The inferior part of creation is this little universe. Let us see what we mean by 'physical universe'. You must not think we are talking about our earth, or even our cosmic system; we are talking about everything that exists as a physical reality any where in space. We are talking just as much about the undiscovered stars as about the earth on which we live. The physical nature of existence - everything in space that has a form. When we say 'physical', we mean Form. We know that form exists not only in the things you can see; but in things you can catch through hearing, for example. Form is not simply the physical object you see; you cannot see a word, yet a word is a form. a thought is a form. In the inferior universe we include all states and conditions of form; form includes every part of nature below the level of thought.

Rates of consciousness above the thinking process are given a different name than form; what is below is a part of the form world. Our feelings are forms; our thoughts are forms; our bodies are forms, and every part of form is the 'Circle' in our symbolism. Form is often symbolized by the skeleton; the emblem of death. Consciousness lies buried in Form. In form all life is inhibited; no creature who is controlled by the form part of itself is rational. The ultimate degree of form is ultimate negation, philosophically, because it is the absence of all that is necessary to the greatest good of the greatest number. In form, in its ultimate state, life is at its lowest ebb; form is well called in philosophy the Eternal Adversary; form is to consciousness an imprisoning and limiting agency. Form may be called the world of darkness; the lack of light; form is a condition that lacks awareness - consciousness.

The natural law of Matter is inertia; this is relative inertia. In comparison to the consciousness of man, the active principles of the universe - form or matter is unconscious. The physical universe is that creation in which each of us is at his worst; conquest here is therefore the greatest of all conquest, because it is over the most difficult conditions in life.

In the ancient mysteries Man was taught that his whole universe, considered as one block of substance, was the body of a Great Being, and this Being is called the Lord of Form - the Master of the World. He is called in philosophy the Demiurgus. We do not know just what that means in its original interpretation; but in its physical sense it can be called 'False Urge'. It is the composite material universe, considered as a power - a Being; and this Being is the King of the World and the powers under him are called the Princes of the World. The Princes are the conditions or divisions of the form universe; the Lord of the World is the Autocrat; the philosophic Despot. He controls his universe through fear; he represents the Cycle of Necessity; he controls birth and death.

****

The physical universe, with all its attendant parts, is the sphere with which we are particularly concerned. It is the Deep Sea of Illusion. We are dwelling in it; we know of no other world than the world of darkness. This physical universe is a great Egg, wherein all manners of creatures are passing through their prenatal epoch; we are all embryos; we are not born, until we are born out of the egg of darkness; we are living in a world as dark and mysterious as the world in which we exist in the embryonic period.

Alchemy says there is gold in everything; philosophy says there is a rational soul in everything. Alchemy says by a mysterious formula the gold can be extracted and be made to grow and increase; philosophy says that the rational soul, by a certain method, can be brought out of the base nature, growing and bearing fruit. Alchemy says when you have the combinations of chemicals properly prepared you begin the cycle of distillation and you gradually cause the chemicals to pass through cycles of increasing intensity; finally you reach a point where the elixir - the rational soul - sees right through the glass of the globe or retort. The cycles of intensification represent the processes of human regeneration; the rational soul of man seeps through the shell of irrationality; that is the projection of the Philosopher's Stone. When the cycles reach a certain point the glass will no longer hold the elixir; when the soul of man has reached a certain degree of unfoldment the walls of physical matter can no longer hold him and he escapes. The philosophic birth is out of the Egg of Matter - out of illusion, into reality.

There are two births and two deaths of every individual. There is the birth of consciousness into matter; it is simply cosmic death; everything that is born into form dies in formlessness. Every birth into material existence passes out of a greater state into a lesser state. This is a philosophic birth; the philosophic birth is the immersion of a rational soul into the irrational universe. The individual is born in and out of conditions of reality; all in The Egg itself. There is the philosophic death, which is the escape of the rational soul, out of the irrational soul, forever.

****

The physical universe can only control substance like itself. There is something in every one of us that is not physical; science can call it force, energy, life - whatever it wants to; its sojourn in matter is simply that it may learn the workings of the universe. Now comes the question: just how does man escape this spell and what makes it possible? It is the positing of consciousness. Man lives where his thoughts are; the universe that he knows is simply the universe to which his thinking is attuned. When man, as a divine being, is willing and accepts the illusionary universe, he is swallowed up in it. Man is made up of many parts; a divine part (the Dot) a super-human part (the Line) and a natural part (the Circle). When controlled by his physical propensities he is bound to the material universe. When he lives in the world of his higher thinking he then dwells in the intellectual sphere; when he lifts his mind to spiritual realization then he lives in the spiritual world; therefore the world we live in is simply the world wherein we have centered our activities. The higher our ideals - the higher our activities, the higher the world we live in.

Selfishness is the key to the Inferno; the physical world is controlled and directionalized by selfishness. As long as selfishness is in the soul that individual is held to the world of selfishness; we have our own nature within that binds us to a corresponding world without. The moment the qualities within ourselves are changed we ascend into new worlds of qualities outside ourselves. For this reason man is held by his materiality to a material sphere; by his intellectuality to an intellectual sphere; by his ideality to the ideal sphere; but he is continually bound by his innate reality to the reality of existence.

When man masters materiality and there is no longer materiality within himself, then philosophically he is free from the material world. As soon as the intellectuality within himself is transmuted into ideality, he passes from a world of thinking to a world of idealization. While physically he may not appear to change - the world man lives in is made of the stuff he thinks and feels with. The philosophic ascension of the soul is simply the raising of the method, concept and process of living.

From the circumference of materiality he passes to the line of intellectualism; from the line of intellectualism he passes to the dot of spiritual understanding; and lastly he finds the spirit itself is outgrown; and from the dot he is resolved into the blank piece of paper. Growth is the rising out of; the outgrowing of; growth is an increase of understanding in which the soul learns to slough off the least and grasp the best; continually ascending, casting off limitation after limitation. These limitations are not cast off by the process of turning from responsibility; they are cast off by the mastery of environment. There is no success but complete mastery.

****

Lecture # 4

POTENTIALITIES AND POTENCIES

Manly P. Hall   6/1/1928

Unpublished Pages of "*The Secret Teachings of All Ages*"

LECTURES BY MANLY P. HALL   NO. 4
                                                                        6/1/?

                        POTENTIALITIES AND POTENCIES
                        ─────────────────────────────

        The first thing this evening we want to call to your attention is the
difference between potentialities and potencies; potentialities are possibilities;
potencies are actualities. A potential power is a form of power not awake, or not
distinct; for example, in the acorn there is a potential oak tree, but when the oak
tree has grown the potentialities in the seed become active, manifesting principles -
potencies.

        Man is a combination of potentialities and potencies; man is made up of a
limited number of active powers and an unknown number of potentialities or latent
possibilities. The universe, like man, is composed of potentialities and potencies.
By the process of unfoldment, possibilities are ever becoming objective realities. Every
day some potentiality in us becomes a potency; we are like seeds, containing within
ourselves possibilities unnumbered.

        Our first problem this evening is a series of analogies based upon the Tree.
The tree is peculiarly appropriate as an emblem of unfolding potentiality; a tree is
composed of certain distinct parts, and for our philosophy this evening we must imagine
the universe to be a tree. Let us analyze the nature of the universe as a tree.

        The first point (the Dot) established in the fields of Space is the Seed of
the World Tree. In that first seed germ was contained all that has ever come out of it;
countless worlds hurling through space; all that has ever been - all that ever will be -
in potentiality. When a seed begins to grow certain things take place; first the roots
descend; then the stem ascends; gradually stalks - growth unfolds and potentialities are
transmuted into active powers. The trunk of the tree, then the greater branches - each
going its proper way; upon the branches come smaller branches, then the twigs, leaves,
blossoms, and then the new seed germ - the whole life is from one acorn. Some time, in
infinite progression, the one first acorn becomes uncounted billions of acorns - from one
just like them. Every acorn to the end of time, was in the FIRST acorn.

        If you can appreciate the relationship of all the acorns to the first primitive
one, you can begin to understand the possibilities of Space; from one atom can all space
be filled. Space, the great potentiality, is made up of infinite numbers - abstract in
the extreme - units of existence. The monad, so small in its beginnings, there is no
possible mental conception of them - has enough activity within it to ultimately fill
space with its outpourings and manifestations.

        This brings a train of circumstances: the minute potentialities are capable
of evolving into universes if they secure the proper environment. Until the water and
light strike them they are barren. A dry grain of wheat contains a germ of life, among
its multitude of potentialities; these germs do not grow until the proper environment and
impulse is supplied. They remain monads; out of them is composed the substance of Space.
If we could conceive the nature of space, we would see here and there, among that mass of
particles, a flash - a fire - and a monad starts to grow; why - philosophy does not know.
Only one thing is known; this growth continues and unfolds. The monad as a simple cell,
simple form of life, gradually expands from within outward; gradually manifests its
potentialities; and can be likened to a tree.

NC. 5

We are going to imagine the seeds have been planted in space, and have come up. Gradually from the little monad is growing forth the universe. At various periods in the process of the unfoldment of this great plan new lives begin to express themselves; it is discovered this one monad, which contains within itself the power of reproduction, (cell fission) begins the process of breaking up into more monads - until structure is established. Every human being was first a primitive cell - increasing in complexity until the complete individual is produced. Man is just as much the 'first cell' as he is the complete body.

We have around us examples of how the cell swells; by Force - always it is moved outward by the potentialities within itself. So the tree grows, but never beyond the limit of the first cell. The highest expression of the growth of the germ is the reproduction of the cell; the perfection of the tree lies in its ability to create its own kind. When the tree has completed its life, in the production of acorns, it declines; gradually the tree disappears because it is absorbed, so to speak, in the acorns it has produced, and the tree goes on in the germs that come from it. The life in the tree continues on, becoming the life of all trees produced from it.

We find in the tree a very good symbol with which to establish the nature of existence; but the thing this is leading up to is this: when we define the Absolute as All there Is, we then define it as the sum of the expressions of Itself. We dare to presume something; the Absolute is the sum of all there is in the nature of infinite potentiality, but the Absolute in its nature may be likened to the acorn, which is the sum of all that will ever come out of it - yet, like the acorn, it is capable of increasing continually and eternally. We believe in ascribing to Perfection the state of increase. Perfection and the Absolute is all there is; but 'Is' is ever becoming more. We must consider the Absolute in terms of absolute potentiality, capable of producing out of itself an infinitude of ever-evolving individualities. Consequently the sum of all is continually increasing.

* * * * * *

We have been working with the Dot, the Line and the Circle - working from the Dot outward. A symbol must also work in two ways: from the circumference inward. It is another way of figuring growth. Absolute consciousness or spirit is not only in the center working outward; but it is in the circumference, working inward. Ask a philosopher where spirit in man is, and he would probably tell you it is in the heart; if you were a disciple he would tell you the true seat of it was in the atmosphere around you - in the circumference - concentrating on the center.

The Self is the All. When you have reached a certain position in philosophy you realize the Self is not the center in you, but is centered in Space. You, as the 'I Am', is not the Self. The Self permeates everything; it is not individualized in one person. "IN" is towards Self; Out is away from Self; The individual who goes towards the Center of Real Being goes outward; growth is from form to formlessness. 'Inward' is from personality to Principle; 'Outward' - away from Self - is from principle to personality As long as man functions in form he must grow. Liberation is the escape of consciousness from limitation.

* * * * *

Lecture # 5

DIFFERENCES BETWEEN KNOWLEDGE AND BELIEF

Manly P. Hall   6/2/1928

Unpublished Pages of "*The Secret Teachings of All Ages*"

LECTURES BY MANLY P. HALL   NO. 5

DIFFERENCES BETWEEN KNOWLEDGE AND BELIEF

We want to continue the point of realization or understanding. We began last evening with the hypothetical target of concentric rings to show the way the soul in man grows. We must further realize something else, and that is: the secret of the relationship between form and the growing life. If man's spiritual nature is continually increasing we will find the ultimate result in a complete separation between the spiritual and material constitutions. The human body is in reality a groundwork upon which an infinite number of lives are evolving; it is inhabited by a great number of races of living things - from cells to vast organisms, which are self-sustaining forms. There are races of cells, and whole tribes of cells that together make one certain part of the body; another mass of cells will be of an entirely different kind; they depend on man for their life in the same way we depend upon the sun for ours. Each individual furnishes a different type of environment to the development of cell life. A very highly evolved cell life comes into incarnation where the condition of the human body furnishes and supplies the proper setting. As man, through his growth, his philosophy, his idealism, increases and heightens the vibratory rate of his own body, he furnishes environments for higher forms of life; this is the refinement of substance. It results in higher rates of life coming into manifestation as parts; the cell structure of his brain becomes of a better quality - more finely organized. The individual transmutes the substance of his body into a spiritual essence.

Let us consider the difference between fact and belief. The world is ruled by beliefs; men are servants to their attitudes, their beliefs. Standards of right and wrong are beliefs. One Fact gives to the individual who possesses it, absolute power. When an individual knows something his strength is equal to his knowing, and his weakness is about equal to his belief. Text books are aggregations of beliefs. How is it possible to change belief for knowledge? Then comes the great test; namely, there is no such thing as second-hand knowledge; when it becomes second-hand, it becomes a belief. Vision, or knowledge, cannot be communicated, bought, sold or exchanged; it is not a commodity. Knowing is an interval of realization; nor can the nature of it be communicated. Each person must himself become a Knower. Knowledge is borne out of you; beliefs are hung onto you. Knowledge is within; beliefs come from the without. It is knowledge of the individual that picks up the rest of humanity and sweeps it with them, for man cannot resist the power of it. Knowledge is realization - an innate knowledge is innate realization of a fact.

The Greek mysteries were devoted to the process of initiating men and women into the mysteries of life. Any one who knows any one great truth is an initiate. The difference between the inner and the outer is the difference between belief and knowledge. Initiations continue, each new initiation giving Man a new fact. Man's reward to the Knower is persecution. The Greek philosophers were capable of assisting man to know; they had the secret processes whereby to assist man to secure knowledge. The mastery of death was one of the first facts; remember that in philosophy immortality is not the perpetuation of a physical body; but is the realization of the incorruptibility of The Self.

NO. 6

The Knower is the Dot; the fact is the circle; the faculty of knowing is the Line that connects them. The Dot is noumena; the Circle, the phenomena. The Arts are peculiarly powerful media between the Knower and things to be known because in art we have a number of methods of expression which are not generally possible in words; and although a person may be a great orator - a picture will awaken responses that words do not bring out. The Arts therefore connect the Knower and the things known. The interval between the knower and the thing to be known is diminished and finally annihilated by the effort to understand. This interval is bridged in three ways; the creative manifestation of the heart, the mind and the hand; through Wisdom, through learning, man learns to know; through love, feeling, man learns to feel or feels to know; through service of his fellowmen, through labor, man works to know. There are three paths that lead to a fact; the intellectual (mind), the aesthetic (heart) and the physical (the hand in labor). That which we build with our hand (symbol of physical propensities) brings with it an understanding of the thing labored with (knowledge of a fact). Through service man finds his God in his world. The first path is the path of the server; this is the physical road. There is the second road - the path of Love, in which the highest expression of love is gained - by the transmutation of passion to compassion. (Knowledge gained through feeling). In the deepest and most profound feelings of the human soul there lies a hidden road - leading from belief to fact. If life be controlled by the highest emotions, reality is found in the thing loved. The loves of individuals grow into the love of worlds; in the finest and fullest expression of human emotion is found a certain road to the discovery of a fact.

The third - the mental knower - the one who has found reality or a fact by the avenue of thought. By thought vistas of abstract space have been conquered. By means of the mind unrealities have been detected and the realities discovered. Some walk by one path, some by another. Some have found facts who never read a book. The first step to the completeness of spiritual and individual consciousness is the discovery of a fact.

So train the feelings of your heart, so train the faculties of your reasoning powers, and the skill of your fingers that all three shall be primarily concerned with the principles in things, and not the forms in which those principles are imprisoned. When we begin to look for principles we will find facts Through clear thinking, in its noblest sense; through fine feeling, in its finest aspect; through diligence, in the labor of life, we gradually learn facts. All of this is simply a process where - by cosmic urge - we are compelled to exchange our beliefs for facts When we have learned how to live we are through with life; when we have learned the mystery of life then we pass to a nobler sphere, and our labor is to learn to know.

****

Lecture # 6

THE DISCIPLINE OF FACTS

Manly P. Hall   6/3/1928

Unpublished Pages of "*The Secret Teachings of All Ages*"

LECTURES BY MANLY P. HALL   NO. 6

THE DISCIPLINE OF FACTS

(The Divine Principle - impersonal, transcending limitation and description, is the only God philosophy recognizes. An Eternal Principle - standing for the sum of All that exists - as the object of all existence, and as the subject of all existence. Any conception that is less than the absolute ultimate of Beauty and Goodness, is not worth bothering about).

*****

A flexible intellect is absolutely necessary to growth. Pythagoras was probably the greatest of the Greek philosophers, although less known than Plato and Aristotle. The first thing that was great in his teachings was the fact that he established certain disciplines by means of which the mind of man was elevated to the point where it was capable of thinking - of having a thought. A thought so well constructed that it can stand analysis. Thinking is just as difficult and just as exact a science as any other science in the world. It is just as necessary to have training in thinking as in medicine, law, astronomy, etc. Intelligent thinking and a knowledge of right and wrong do not come to people naturally. It is learned by a definite process of procedure. Knowledge of right and wrong is brought out from the depths of the soul (latent within) or else it must be learned through rational thinking; rational thinking is an exact process - a process as scientific as any of the arts or sciences.

We come now to disciplines of philosophy. The individual comes to learn how to think; it is more difficult today to secure the knowledge of how to think, because we only teach what to think. In the Pythagorean school the great philosopher either instructed, or moulded by his philosophy, over 1000 people. The first thing Pythagoras asked the student was: 'What do you know?' He demanded knowledge of three things: mathematics, music and astronomy. To those who desired to become philosophers the disciplines of these three are absolutely indispensable. What does it mean to become proficient in these three? The knowledge of these three great branches of learning give the necessary foundation for thinking.

If all the physical universe is illusionary, what is the purpose of study? The illusion is all the negative expression of cosmic forces. To master the illusion it is necessary to analyze the fabric of the illusion; this is best attained through these three sciences. Through mathematics the mind is trained in the most primitive and and the most divine of all sciences; it is the beginning of all knowing. When people realize that the whole fabric of the universe is permeated with exact principles they begin to think in terms of exactness. Without mathematics - nothing else can be known. All other arts and sciences are dependencies of mathematics, -The Dot in our symbolism. Music is the Line and Astronomy the circle. Spiritual Mathematics (The One); the Supreme Name of God; Mental Harmonics (The Beautiful - force moving outwards); Physical Dynamics (the science of the relationship of energies in Space). Study Mathematics. The Platonic solids are the greatest single aid to the understanding of philosophy.

Astronomy shows the mind the proper subject for thought; you will find the stars are great universes, and the earth a speck. It gives us the sense of magnitude - and furthermore, the magnitude of the power that is controlling the universe.

NO. 7
6/4/28

Philosophy is concerned with infinites and ultimates. Philosophy is not a cold thing; it is very much like a wise parent; it chastises because it loves. The great philosopher is the noblest, kindest of all men; with the depth of understanding comes an infinite regard, love and tenderness; most of all is born a vast comradeship. In philosophy we gerneralize. The sparks of Infinite Being have discovered they are together here; they are on a great caravan route through space, marching through the aeons; philosophy believes that each of these sparks should hold out its hand to the next little spark and they all should march on together. Philosophy is the creed of the honest man. Mental honesty. The fellowship of those who understand marches on through the ages; they are the ones who have taught man through and for love of man; they give their lives to serve man.

There is something in the human heart as great as Law. That something else is Compassion. If it dies it leaves nothing worth while. So while we must apply the Law to ourselves, we must be filled with compassion for our fellows. We, in our own hearts and souls become, in time, masters of law; we come to understand - and it is not that we learn to break the law but through the compassion of the wise we learn to live better with the law. Universality of divine law - to continuously do all we can to help the other fellow how to live according to that law. The knowledge of the law is not enough; everything we know we become temporarily keepers of; that means that every bit of knowledge we secure we become responsible for; to see that it shall do the greatest good to the greatest number.

****

Lecture # 7

OBSERVATION
DISCRIMINATION
CONCENTRATION

Manly P. Hall   6/4/1928

Unpublished Pages of "*The Secret Teachings of All Ages*"

LECTURES BY MANLY P. HALL   NO. 7
                                                                            6/4/28

OBSERVATION - DISCRIMINATION - CONCENTRATION

What does observation mean? Observation means the power of seeing the thing you are looking at. You do not merely fasten your eye on a thing, but your eye takes in the elements of that object and your brain becomes immediately aware of the object intelligently. Sight is given to man that he may see.

In symbolism and in philosophy observation is absolutely necessary because the great truths are always concealed, and in some way are made difficult of access; and it is only to the individual who is observing that can see the ting guide marks given to aid in the discovery of truth itself. Great truths are always retiring; consequently it is only the individuals who look deeply that find. For four centuries it has been customary to mark all books that contain the Secret Doctrine; the mark is there; people who see do not find it; people who observe, find it. It is almost akin to X-Ray vision - to grasp the importance of the hidden symbol.. (Read the italicized words in Mr Hall's book; learn to observe - look for the hidden mark).

Observation is that faculty which sees so thoroughly that the simplest and apparently most insignificant thing is immediately noted. Observation is more than that; it is the ability to see the reality of things; seeing into, through and behind things. It is the ability to differentiate between form and life. He who observes can find faintly visible the principles moving form; observation is that faculty that enables man to discover wisdom. (Nature is the Book of Holy Writ; but it takes the eye of observation to see all the parts of it together; from observation man becomes master of knowledge).

Learning and knowledge are not the same thing; learning is to beg, borrow or steal the thought of others; knowing is to think yourself. A learned person knows what other people think; a knowing person is an individual who knows what he thinks himself; learning is communicated by others; knowledge is evolved within the self.

After observation has brought to the attention of the reasoning faculties a mass of phenomena, then comes the next great power - discrimination. How few have it - and how vital it is! Man knows that in one short span of physical life he cannot know everything; he cannot have everything; he cannot be everything; but discrimination will assist him to choose from the things that he _may_ have the things he _should_ have; and discrimination will assist him in choosing from that which is - that which is _first_. Discrimination is the faculty of arranging things in comparative order; organized steps of valuation. It enables man to accomplish the most in any particular period of time; any particular type of work. Discrimination, in the thought of the Greek philosophers, is that faculty which organizes things into numerical sequences; first the First - then the second, etc. Discrimination is the most precious possession of the inferior nature of man, for by means of it he is able to conserve time, energy, thought, life - and man has what he saves - and loses what he wastes. It is the basis of a proper conservation of life; the length of our life is measured by the number of things we accomplish; accomplishment, and not time, is the measure of existence. Wisdom and knowledge - these are the supreme accomplishments - and discrimination is the power which weeds out the unnecessary elements and leaves the impulses and intellect of the individual free to concern itself with the most important matters.

There are three kinds of discrimination; first, the discrimination which reveals - of a number of physical objects or conditions - the most important (which is first - which secondary). There is a second form of discrimination which is concerned with the relative integrity - the innate goodness of things. To detect the relative merits, or moral construction of things. The third form is the innate ability to detect reality and illusion (as to which is the Real Man - the physical or the spiritual constitution of man).

(People must choose their ethical and philosophical outlook of life; they must learn to discriminate between people and what they do; between the thinker and his thought; between the spirit and his body; between the innate divinity within and the objective materiality without). Discrimination lifts the consciousness of the individual until he perceives only the best in things; seeing within the body - spirit. And most of all the ability to see Self in everything. While selfishness exists, discrimination can not; discrimination is helpless until man becomes honest mentally with himself.

Discrimination is further involved in the problem of the choice of activities for the mind, for the body; it is concerned with the choice of the best objects to think about; with the ability to choose the things in life with which you can do something. It is thus serviceable to us in our effort to complete the parts of ourselves; it assists us to develop the power to cope with life activities by first discovering them. It is one of the most beautiful faculties that can possibly be awakened in the soul of man; it has, as its ultimate example of perfection, the realization of the complete and infinite goodness of things.

The Spirit in man is always beautiful; discrimination is the ability to recognize the real self in things; the recognition of that self is synonomous with the realization of the divinity of self. We find what relationship, physically, really means; a relationship is a man-made idea of the distance between things; relationship is man's effort to separate things. In the depth of philosophy there is a realization that the 'Brother and I' are 'One'. Discrimination reveals but one relationship, and all the rest is an illusion of the mortal mind. The one relationship is a complete synchronizing of the two selves - spiritually we are One.

Ignorance is analytical and analyzes. Wisdom synthesizes or brings together. Discrimination proves the impossibility of hate (ignorance); it is the key to reality and illusion; it uses certain weapons - that which is real is conscious - is synthetic - is unified; that which is unreal is separate, unconscious and diversified.

From the stage of discrimination we rise to the subject of concentration. The Aryan race is not able to concentrate. We think of concentration as a mental one-pointedness; it includes physical and emotional pointedness to the same point. Concentration is the power that carries man to accomplishment. Having discovered what is right - what he will do - the purpose of his life, by observation and discrimination, man determines to attain, and attains through concentration. It is the focalising of all energies on the task at hand. To concentrate means to have the mind stay with a subject. In life - to remain with its purpose and goal until it achieves. There is a philosophical saying that 'Once a man has discovered the thing he wants to do, or to be, that through the mind's focalization on that point he can ultimately accomplish anything he desires to accomplish'. We find that the mind becomes absorbed in the thing upon which it has concentrated continuously and conscientiously; if he wants, consistently, to attain to any condition of knowing, he will attain. Concentration is the setting of the life upon the path of accomplishment; once man discovers reality it will become his goal; man accomplishes according to his power of concentration. Mental and spiritual activity, focalized on a central point, will bring attainment.

NO. 8
6/5/28

Without these three great tools of power man will not know the value of his beliefs (observation); will not know the order of his beliefs (discrimination) and will never accomplish his beliefs (concentration). If these three are used conscientiously and consistently togwther they will liberate man to the service of ideals, and will help the student to realize the purpose of life - and having realized it, will give him the strength to attain that purpose. Concentration is the Dot; discrimination the Line; observation the Circle.

****

Lecture # 8

RELATIONSHIP OF SYMBOLISM TO THE HUMAN BODY

Manly P. Hall   6/5/1928

Unpublished Pages of "*The Secret Teachings of All Ages*"

LECTURES BY MANLY P. HALL

NO. 8

RELATIONSHIP OF SYMBOLISM TO THE HUMAN BODY

It will be necessary to call your attention to the favorite analogy of antiquity. The nature of the universe is best to be estimated by the consideration of the nature of Man. In ancient philosophy creation was a gigantic individual, and man was the 'little individual'. We are confronted with an apparent contradiction, because we have been calling your attention to the fact that the creative powers should not be considered as personalities; but it is necessary - to be able to understand and to relate these apparent contradictions. In symbology man is as much an abstract being as the universe; symbolism does not consider man a personality, but man as a composite being - made of an infinite number of parts - gathered together and controlled by a unit of consciousness, which - in turn - is a fragment of the universal consciousness.

This brings us to another question; viz: the exact purpose of symbols. You must realize that a physical symbol is created to impress the holder with a quality. Symbols are not made to reveal form, but qualities. A hand, in symbolism, represents a quality - the thing that it represents may not have form at all - but it may have five qualities and therefore the fingers are an appropriate symbol for it. Symbolism is the language by means of which the Formless agents or principles are reduced to form, or are expressed in the qualities of form. Which means that a symbol is a crystilization of an abstract principle; an effort to find something in nature that is superior to nature. Symbolism is the effort to endow abstract qualities with tangible forms consistent with the innate constitution of the thing symbolized.

Form is nothing more nor less than the objectification, in matter, of certain qualities of life or life activity. A human body is simply a symbol of the unfoldment of consciousness. All forms are symbols and represent the condition of the life manifesting through the form. Every machine is a symbol of a mechanical principle, crystalized into form. Man must be instructed not only in the physical phenomena that he sees around him but in the abstract, moral, metaphysical, and spiritual qualities; it is absolutely necessary to employ symbols to understand the formless.

Symbolism is the most profound form of learning in the world, and symbols depend upon correspondences. You say: 'It is like that, and yet it is not that'. Symbols may be physical emblems; they may be word pictures; they may be color and tone values; they may be thought pictures of something that is not words, and yet you can get something, in part, the thing symbolized.

We will pass on to the subject of our Man, in symbolism. There is a correspondence between the functioning organism of an individual, and the functioning organism of the whole; this is the supreme secret - the fact that he who understands the workings of himself understands the workings of the Whole. He who understands or comprehends the workings in full, of the little cell - will understand the workings of the Universal Being; there are correspondences in the nature of the two. If we can apply these laws we are then on the road to the use of symbols, properly.

That this truth, concerning the mystery of the human body as an image of Universal Being - an abstract philosophical concept - that this might be preserved for all time, every great temple of antiquity was built upon a plan that was furnished by the human body. When they built a temple in the form of man they did not limit it to the physical man, but the composite man - spiritual, mental and physical; all of the parts of man were arranged symbolically as the parts of truth.

Symbols do not always reveal themselves instantly; they are like the leaves of the cabbage - you have to pick one after another before you find the heart of the cabbage; you will find in studying symbolism that one symbol reveals another more abstract and as consciousness of man reaches the point where it can unveil them, he will arrive at an understanding of the heart.

In man there is the supreme life agent - the proper subject and object of veneration; consequently there is no more fitting shrine than man; for his various natures are to his spirit what a cathedral might be to a God who is presumed to dwell in the sanctuary. In every form there is an 'Inner Room' which is the dwelling place of the hidden spirit; the Universe is a great temple; in it is a hidden room which only the wise can discover, and in this room dwells the Hidden God - The One who is ever revealed, but but ever-concealed; 'revealed in creation, but concealed in essence'. In the midst of every body is the Holy of Holies; in the human life there is the innder Holy of Holies - man's spiritual part, which is the Inner Room; his physical part is the Outer Room, and the Inner Room is within the Outer Room.

Having conceived the spirit of man to dwell in the hidden place of him, it is next necessary to realize that ancient adage: 'The spirit of man is a three-phased (3-faced) God'. The spirit being the ultimate of life, is the ultimate of the three great expressions of existence; Will, which is consciousness; Wisdom, which is intelligence, and Action, which is force. All of these together equal all life. Life is the undivided form; the phases are consciousness, action and intelligence.

If we view the nature of physical man we realize that, physically, there are three important centers in his physical constitution; three cardinally important centers. The three most valuable things in his body are the heart, brain and reproductive system. While all parts of him are necessary, these three are presumed to be, in philosophy, the most important parts of man; the part by which he IS; the part by which he thinks; and the part by which he perpetuates himself. It is proper that we should posit consciousness in the heart - the power to live. The heart has life in it. The heart represents, in philosophy, consciousness - it is the symbol of consciousness because it is recognized as the center of physical consciousness. It is the state of being alive; it is the Father-principle; it is Life.

The Intelligence - wisdom - the Son of Life - the Light (real intelligence is the power that glorifies life), is the second attribute of Divine Being; it is capable of becoming aware of the magnitude of the plan. It is, symbolically, posited in the brain because wisdom has its tiny reflection in the human intelligence.

Force is activity; the universe has a physical active nature; there is the energy that is continually moving the globes of space. The generative power is represented as the active principle of God. No where do we find divine activity more magnificently revealed than in the process of building forms for the manifestation of life. This cosmic activity, physical generation, is the least of the three manifesting principles; because it is concerned entirely with Form. The Dot is Consciousness (cosmic Will to Create - masculine); the Line is the Intelligence (Phallic principle - feminine or Mother aspect); the Circle is the active principle (symbol of the world matrix in which universes are cast).

NO. 9
6/5/28

You will find there are two ways of expressing dignity; the most common puts that most dignified on top; the common practice in symbolism is to put the most exalted object on top – or at the farthest end. Although consciousness is in the human heart it is the highest point in his nature and is therefore exalted to the head in symbolism because it is the highest part of the body. The head is the superior part and to dignify consciousness it is presumed to be in the head. But philosophically there is a point more exalted than the head – and that is the center. The center wherein the Self dwells – the point of absolute balance – of equilibrium; that is truly the dignified spot. Consciousness is placed, exterically, in the head; but esoterically, in the heart.

****

THE TEMPLE

SPIRIT in CONSCIOUSNESS

(Circular dome; the Light of the Sun enters the body of man through the soft spot in the top of the head)

Outer Room
the BODY

Intelligence is the method by which man reaches Consciousness

The devotee enters the body of the building (Seven steps leading up to the door or entrance represent the seven planes of the lower or physical universe by which man climbs to intelligence. These represent Activity)

After man has climbed the seven steps – physical activity – he then enters the intellectual plane (a disciple of wisdom). When he has passed to the Inner, he IS Wisdom. Wisdom becomes incarnate in those who have attained Wisdom.

Lecture # 9

RELATIONSHIP OF SYMBOLISM TO MAN (II)

Manly P. Hall   6/6/1928

Unpublished Pages of "*The Secret Teachings of All Ages*"

LECTURES BY MANLY P. HALL

NO. 9
6/6/28

RELATIONSHIP OF SYMBOLISM TO MAN

(Continued)

The three great divisions of the microcosm, the lesser universe, we declared to be correlated with the symbolism of the heart, the brain and the reproductive system. These three centers of power represent the divine agents, or life principles, reflected into physical matter. It is very evident that the brain of man is not the thinking part - the brain is simply the vehicle of the thinker, and thoughts are shadowed on the brain. Remove the life principle from man and the brain ceases to think, although, physically, it is not greatly changed. The heart of man is a physical organ - is simply a physical body, moved by an internal spiritual power. It is also true that the generative part of the human body is simply the physical shadow of a spiritual agency. The heart, the brain and generative system are simply physical forms - the shadows, as it were, of spiritual principles.

As man's consciousness controls all of his body, so there is, in the heart, a consciousness which, in the correspondence of consciousness of man - occupies the same position his spirit does. In our symbolism we said that a symbol is simply a form used to represent a formless principle; therefore, the heart is used to represent the formless principle of life, because physically the heart is the center of life. It is the part of physical nature most attuned to consciousness.

****

Wherever we have in symbolism a magnified organ, it represents an added or spiritual activity of that part; the arm or hand of the eastern Deities are often very numerous; no one should presume that the Oriental believes God had that many arms; they are emblematic of powers. (The Hand - would be emblematic of labor or activity; God, the All-Powerful One, is the Eye (who neither sleeps nor slumbers). God, the Creator, is the Hand. The various members of the body - the foot, the hand, the eye, all represent the efforts to assign symbols appropriate to attributes).

There comes with this a further thought; that all of the deities of antiquity represent states of consciousness. Whenever an individual attains to that state of consciousness which the God symbolizes then it is considered a God is incarnate in that personality. In the Temple of the 10,000 Buddhas you will find a limitless number of images of Bodhisattvas - or disciples of the Lord of Enlightenment; these simply represent stages or conditions of enlightenment. Here we have, for example; Kwan Yan - Goddess of Mercy - a female figure with six arms; one arm is with the head leaning in it; one of these holds a staff; another holds images, etc. Whoever gives anything - for the pleasure of giving - is presumed to give with the hand of Kwan Yan; for a moment when the individual gives it is said to have the consciousness of Kwan Yan; in this western world we would say the individual has a generous streak - it is a degree of consciousness that finds joy in giving. Another hand is the joy of receiving; not only giving, but receiving, brings a realization of life. This is a symbol - a personality created to represent the element of generosity. The proper image of such qualities is a noble one; the Kwan Yan is a condition of the Self, and when man rises to the heights where he loves to give, to serve, and to lift others to realization - when the soul attains that condition - then, in the east, the 'Kwan Yan' is born.

Every individual has a complete pantheon of world deities within himself, and as his realization rises, he is ruled by these - one after another, until he reaches the highest. Gradually man rises from the relationship of one to the relationship of another, until he ultimately accomplishes liberation.

There are three main divisions of realization; physical realization, mental realization, spiritual realization. These three are divided into an infinite number of subdivisions; but man is one of three things - he is either ruled by his body, by his mind or else he rules them both. When man is ruled by his physical nature he is called a materialist - and in mastery over his inferior parts, appetites and desires - he achieves completeness. From attachment to physical objects, man ascends to a higher plane, and becomes enmeshed in mind; finally, after ages of suffering, man frees himself and rises to the mastery of both the mind and the body; when he rules the mind and the body he becomes a rational creature.

******

There are our three worlds, ruled by three Suns - represented in the human body by the heart, the pineal gland and the prostatic gland. Concerning the nature of these three worlds in man - it is presumed, in philosophy, that every center of power is surrounded by a radiant nimbus of light. In the heart of man there is a radiance of light; this radiance is a globe, with its upper end touching the pineal gland, its lower touching the prostatic gland; one globe uniting three centers of consciousness. This is symbolic; you cannot see it. There are forces that achieve that symbolic form. The pineal gland is a center of radiant power - a little seed of flaming fire, surrounded by this nimbus of light. It extends upward out of the head, and downward to the heart - making another globe. In the third center we have again the flame; again the globe - reaching upward to touch the heart; the center globe touching all three - the other two touching two centers. These three are the fire or consciousness units in a human body; these are positive and negative, according to certain activity in human life. The materialist who lives in his animal nature so accentuates the lower pole of power that it increases in power, becoming positive; therefore, in the materialist this disc around the pineal gland is negative and around the heart it is negative; but around the generative system is positive - controlling the emotions of the heart. In the intellectualist the pineal gland becomes positive; the heart is controlled by the mind and is negative; the generative system is negative; the mind controls the activity.

When the individual assumes the higher life - the life of consciousness - gradually the heart center begins to become positive; the mind and the generative system both become negative; the central disc becomes more powerful until it touches both extremes and are controlled by the central consciousness. This is a diagrammatic explanation of the human unfoldment and mastery.

****

Try to picture a human body with these three points: (1) Brain (2) Heart and (3) Generative System - imagine a human figure for each point - they are the Trinity. The heart of man is the chief part of his body; it compares with the Sun in the solar system. We also said that the Sun was the 3rd, or least, power of the Universe - because it is the material light or life and therefore corresponds to the generative system of the Universal Man. The human heart, which is the first part of the consciousness of the body is the least part of the consciousness of the spirit. The spiritual nature of man consists of three parts; the spirit in the heart (which is the basis of the form - the personality of the man; that which is the form building and form maintaining part) is the least of the three aspects of spirit. We have spiritual spirit -

No. 10
6/8/28

intellectual spirit; physical spirit - three aspects; and the heart is the seat of the physical spirit - therefore it is the least part of the spiritual nature; but it is the greatest part of the material nature. The least part of the spirit is the highest part of the human body; consequently we symbolize spirit by an inverted triangle:

```
* * * * * * *
 *         *
  *       *
   *     *     Spirit is a descending power
    *   *         (Away from Self)
     * *
      *
     * *
    *   *
* * * * * *    Matter, crowned by intelligence,
                 is an ascending power.
```

The result being, ultimately, the interlaced triangle - the blending of the spiritual and material natures. Imagine a human body with the apex or point in the heart; and the other two points out of the body and not associated with the physical condition (they have nothing to do with personality). The lower one alone has to do with personality, consequently it is called the Ego, the 'I Am' - the two upper points are called the 'Anthropos' or Overman, and are in no way connected with life or death.

```
                          *
(Spiritual Spirit)   * * * * * *   (Intellectual Spirit)
                      * * * * *
                       * * *
                         *
              (Physical Spirit, in the Heart of Man)
```

When man unfolds, philosophically, he draws these other parts into his consciousness; or rather he rises into theirs. But in the physical life of man, until he rises above his mind, he has no knowledge of the two upper points. His incarnating spirit has, as its highest expression, intellect; and its lowest expression, the form-building power.

****

Lecture # 10

RELATIONSHIP OF SYMBOLISM TO MAN (III)

Manly P. Hall   6/8/1928

Unpublished Pages of "*The Secret Teachings of All Ages*"

LECTURES BY MANLY P. HALL

No. 10
6/8/28

RELATIONSHIP OF SYMBOLISM TO MAN

(Continued)
Part III

God has been defined as the greatest thing an individual can feel, think, know or comprehend; and the materialist finds form sufficiently magnificent to be deified, therefore he worships form; the theologian deifies words - (he gives to the words of certain men a power great enough to elevate these words to a position of absolute infallibility). The philosopher deifies notions, postulations, thoughts and mental processes.

The different attitudes of mind have their foundation in natural tendencies of thinking; every mind that is in exactly the same stage of unfoldment is confronted with exactly the same problems. There is an infinite number of degrees of possible unfoldment; you therefore very seldom find any two minds at the same degree of unfoldment at the same time; every mind of a certain degree of unfoldment is a certain type of intellect. All of the different idiosyncracies of temperament represent degrees of unfoldment in the mind. The mind must be considered as an unfolding unit; it is perfectly natural for some minds to make a certain kind of mistake - every mind has either made, or will make, that mistake in its development, when it passes through that particular stage of development. The individual is the result of the conditions reaped by the intellect.

The mind possesses a vast number of faculty units, and we very seldom find all of these at the same stage; supposing we presume a mind to have 40 faculties - units of potential powers. A mind at the zero stage consists of 40 potentialities - none of them active. The mind at the stage of perfection consists of 40 potencies; the 40 awakened powers. Do you realize how many relations 40 objects can be to each other? So many that it will require 35 ciphers to record.

We have as many possible temperaments as there are relationships or faculties. Let us presume we have 40 faculties and they are all growing together, and are all just even; what would be the natural result? The result would be that every part of the intellect would have equal strength with the other parts of the intellect. This would mean that the individual would be peculiarly capable of judging temperaments because that perfect balance of parts would make the mind capable of understanding an external object in all its different parts and manners and modes - equally. Then we have a perfectly balanced image. In the physical world this person would have no center of interest - there would be nothing that he would excel in over any other thing; there would be conflicting ideas, in which the mind would always be wavering because nothing would be directionalized in any particular way; he could see so many sides of a problem that it would not move in any direction; it would be almost impossible for that mind to attain any proficiency - it would always have against that an equal number of ideas. Raise one faculty a little higher, and you immediately have a one-pointedness - the predominating faculty takes control of the situation.

Philosophically it is presumed that a perfect intellect is one in which the 40 possible faculties are balanced in perfect unfoldment. The complete awakening of all faculties is desirable; but up to that point one predominant faculty is necessary. A wide difference between the development of faculties is fatal. There is something else;

Absolute nature of Man we like to conceive as having the power of 'Increase'. The fullness, becoming fuller and containing always all of the increase of itself. This absolute, unsymbolized, spirit of Man is still the white sheet of paper; it is the unlimited condition into which consciousness moves after the sleep of oblivion. This absolute state of consciousness shares its state with the consciousness of all other creatures. For instance: the animal likewise contains an absolute consciousness, and in this consciousness the consciousness of the animal and of the man differ in quantity, but not in quality. The absolute nature of these things is Identity - in that it had no limitation - and thing which have no limitation in any way are the same as anything else that has absolutely no limitation. The absolute nature, from the qualitative standpoint, of all things, is the same.

First the absolute condition of Space, in its abstract sense, is brought together and considered as a unit under the name of God; or considered as a Being under the general term of Deity; so the absolute life or consciousness of man is focused into what is called Spirit, and Spirit is a certain Dot, established on the face of the Absolute; and the Spirit of Man is the ALL of spiritual nature, considered as the 'One' or the First; the 'Spirit is the First Part of all things'. As Universal Spirit - as The One - breaks up to form the Trinity - so we find the Spirit in Man breaking up upon the cosmic prism - so to speak - and giving first: three primary Rays or Powers which are considered analagous to the Trinity of the Godhead (a three-faced or three-phased God). Of these phases, the first is the spiritual face; the second to a certain degree, the intellective face; and the third, the active phase. The three parts of the spirit are thus represented as: Father Spirit .... Son Spirit
(Spirit) . . (Mind)

. Holy Ghost Spirit
(Body)

Spirit is always Causal; we said Man could be symbolized with the two upper parts of the triangle outside; and the lower point in the heart of man. We use physical intervals of space to represent superphysical degrees of intensity; spiritually the interval between two states of consciousness is a long way apart.

The Fourth Dimension is best expressed by the idea of the use, physically, of an interval of space to represent a superphysical degree of intensity; as we cannot use a fourth dimension and show the 'in-ness' or 'out-ness' of a thing; we have to show it by the relation of another object. Consequently the 4th dimension is the proper measuring rule of intensities and qualities. We separate the things by physical intervals to indicate the difference in their superphysical intensity; the spirit of man is divided into three parts and we make a triangle to show these parts.

The spiritual part of man consists of two over-parts and one incarnating part. When we say 'over' we do not mean 'on top' - we mean an interval of quality, which must be physically symbolized by a physical interval of distance. The over-part was called the 'Over Man' - the Real Man;- that part which involves itself in form is called the incarnating Ego, or, in the Universe, the Third Logos, or Lord of the World. The 'I AM' is the least part of the triangle of Spirit. Superior to this are two over-parts; all of these three parts together constitute One Spirit, and spiritually they are undivided. They occupy the same place at the same time. They are one solid unity; but the three parts of spirit have a qualitative spirit; different in quality, but not in place.

a faculty of the human mind, which is called the power of overshadowing, or control. If this faculty is evolved (it can be, philosophically) all of the faculties of the mind are caused to contribute their part to the quality of thinking.

Elevation of mental power, so that the highest faculties of the mind control the thinking, will result in these faculties supplying the lesser faculties with material to develop themselves. The philosopher is presumed to be one who rules for the people's good; the materialist rules for his own good; the highest faculties of the brain are those which, by ruling the mind, will produce the greatest good for the entire mental structure. We are only good rulers when we accept our responsibilities - when the higher faculties are sufficiently fine in their own structure to see the need of the other faculties, and thus assist in bringing them up to the highest.

The point we wish to bring out is that all of these faculties result in an infinite diversity of temperaments; these temperaments may be either harmonious or inharmonious blendings. From this infinite number of mental combinations are produced an infinite variation of personalities - each thinking according to the adjustment of its own mind - each seeing just as much as its own faculties will reveal. Most minds have predominating, and dominated faculties. The individual cannot - at will - change his thinking; he must do it gradually - by the unfoldment of the thinking apparatus.

****

Man has two sources of knowledge; at least all relative knowledge. One is internal and one is external. It is possible to gather a certain amount of material from one's environment; it is also possible to draw out a certain amount from one's internal constitution, therefore the human consciousness is likened to the Roman God - Janus - the Two-Faced; each in an opposite direction, one inward, and the other outward. Janus is the God of the Month of January, because it faces the old year and it faces the new. Janus represents the spiritual face of man, with two parts - one looking outward to the phenomena; one looking inward, to the noumena, or reality. The height of attainment is when the face which looks inward and the face which looks outward agree in what they see. When the external observation is complemented by the internal realization then we have a high degree of attainment.

****

From this point we will go to the main subject - the problem of our triangle. We know that the triangle is an ancient symbol of God - the Greek letter 'D' - Delta God represents the abstract nature of ALL, symbolized as an active or created Being. God is an imitation of the Absolute; in it is the term of finite existence; God IS - because we have limited the concept of ALL until it becomes a gigantic 'ONE'. When this One, which is Deity, begins to manifest actively potentialities into potencies, we then begin to divide the attributes or activities. We have determined these attributes are three: consciousness, intelligence and force. And we have considered the nature of the Creator as the Dot; the Savior God as the Line and the Holy Spirit as the Circle. All that we have studied concerning the nature of Absolute Being, and the Trinity, let us reduce to the terms of man, and consider the nature of man. We then discover that man, like the Universe, has an absolute spirit - which is neither capable of definition nor limitation - an absolute state of being and consciousness which is neither height not depth, distance nor time - but exists as the Fullness of Dimension - Absolutely Unlimited. This unlimited, immovable, immortal nature of absolute Man possesses but one power which we care to consider with definition; this is the power of extension or expansion.

There is in the heart a little circle of light, which Paracelsus said is equal in size to the last joint of a man's thumb; physically shapeless, representing the incarnating life; it comes into the consciousness at the time of quickening. This flame is the outer flame of the spiritual part; it is the circumference - the 3rd part. Behind (from the standpoint of quality) this flaming ring is the 'Anthropos', or 'Over Man'. The flaming ring is caught in the web of matter (the incarnating spirit) and involved in it, becoming the active principle of matter. The Not-Self dwells in the yellow covering of the heart itself; it is in the outer part - the circumference of the heart. From Spirit, in its incarnating process, come out a mass of evolving agencies which become form.

The so-called body of man, which is nothing but the embryo, is not derived from within but is composed of substances and forces contained in the Egg itself; the body of man is an exudation from within; it is not something we take on; but what we 'ooze out'. There is an invisible 'yolk' which is a resource within our own natures; we manifest outward, internal potentialities in the same way the crustacaen builds its shell. In the same way body comes out of the inner nature - out of the third spiritual part, the Incarnating Ego. (1) Atmic, Divine Creator: (2) Buddhi - the reservoir of materials or resources: (3) the Ego - takes the materials and molds them into form. We have these three points to remember in connection with our spiritual nature; the first part, the Over Man - Guardian of it all; the second part, the Infinite Provider; the third part, the Manifestor, molding into form.

The form, with which we are now concerned, is simply an exudation outward from the internal nature - the second pole of spirit, containing all of the substances which later manifest as physical powers; they are the roots of physical powers. The liberation of man from the condition of involvement in matter is the positing of his consciousness in the higher parts of his Ego. Man rises from form to intelligence; and from intelligence to consciousness; having reached consciousness, he then reaches Nirvana, and the Dot is erased! Consciousness returns again to its First State, PLUS certain things; the PLUS is the thing that makes the ALL grow. The process from Self to Not-Self, and from Not-Self to the Self, is the Wheel of the Law. Dharma is the invincible Law by which Self-hood is attained.

****

Lecture # 11

SYMBOLISM AND RITUALISM

Manly P. Hall   6/9/1928

Unpublished Pages of "*The Secret Teachings of All Ages*"

LECTURES BY MANLY P. HALL

NO. 11
6/9/28

SYMBOLISM AND RITUALISM

We wish to consider primarily the Secret Doctrine contained in ritualism. Most of you have at some time seen some form of ritual, as presented by a secret society or a religious organization. Ritualism is the symbolism which appeals directly to the active sense-perceptions of man. A ritual is usually a symbol composed of living parts; by the actions or motions of people; their regalia; by their robes and by their words - by the formulae of motion and sound, the Secret Doctrine is revealed in ritual - or through the medium of that division of symbolism that is called ritualism. In the 20th century there is a turning away of the mind from ritualism; we are coming to believe the ritual unnecessary. This attitude is largely the result of the fact that ritualism has become empty; and those who go through these meaningless rituals are unaware of the original purpose and are simply acting a prescribed formula - unknown both as to its origin and meaning.

Rituals are not the only form of symbolism that is technically dead. In this twentieth century nearly all symbolism is dead; the science is a lost science. The reason why symbolism, ritualism and allegory are dead is because the modern world is made up of confirmed literalists; we are all of us primarily literalists; the twentieth century is composed very largely of materialists and symbolism cannot survive the attitudes of materialism and literalism.

The death of a symbol means that the true interpretation of it has been lost. No matter how ethical or beautiful the symbol, technically it is of no value if the real meaning is lost. We come to another point in connection with the so-called dead symbols; a symbol, not only is capable of having many interpretations given to it, but as time goes on the symbol itself is changed to meet the interpretations, and consequently is so distorted that its later form is not a true symbol of the original subject.

This brings us to the problem of Source material; if you are interested in a symbol you must trace it back, through its various modifications, until you come as near as you can to the source form of the symbol. You denude it of its incrustations and get down - in part, at least - to the original form. If you can trace the symbol back to its most primitive form you will probably trace it to an understandable point; this results in the necessity of source material. Any symbol over one or two hundred years passes through some modifications; these are almost always the result of trying to conform the symbol into some conceit of the individual handling it.

Another thing that has greatly confused the issue; there are only a certain number of fundamental or First Symbols; the same symbols have been used by vast numbers of people - using them in a different way. Each group uses it to suit their particular doctrine or tenet. The same symbol can be traced in North America and in Asia - giving two schools. This brings us to the migration of symbols; symbols are like migratory birds. You can trace the whole growth of civilization through the migration of symbols. These become of interest to the anthropologists; the migration of symbols is one of the ways in which races and origins are studied by science. Science admits and first discovered two great migratory symbols; the Tau Cross and the Swastika (American symbol traced from Central Asia). The Tau Cross migrated from Egypt; the two crosses are found in South America and both symbols.. These are one of the methods used in checking the migrations from Asia to North America, and the whole development of racial motion has been followed by means of these migrations of symbols. This is another interesting phase of the study of symbolism.

To symbols is also ascribed another peculiarity. They are nearly all of them traceable to one of two sources; either the physical body of man, or the constellations. If we trace them back far enough and denude them of accretions we will discover the purpose and nature of them. The physical symbol is usually worshipped as a proxy of an abstract idea.

* * * * *

Ritualism is a form of symbolism in which the inanimate objects are exchanged for people; and these people are so costumed and accredited with temperaments as to correspond to the more primitive symbols. Ritualism, in itself, is comparatively meaningless - as a closed book, with a string around it has no educational power; but if you open the book and place it in front of an individual who understands and knows how to read, it has power. Ritualism is a book, closed to man. Available to those who are able to read it.

Things are measured in their importance today by their degree of visibility. Symbols and rituals have two origins; either spiritual or material. The symbol either represents a material quality or a spiritual quality. (The Word 'Caesar' is always associated with the idea of 'conquest'). Often symbols are used to shorten the process of communication, and one emblem, universally known and recognized, is used insteead of a lengthy definition or description ('An individual has a mind that sparkles like a diamond'). In the word 'diamond' the individual secures a concept of quality, and understands the person described as 'brilliant'.)

In symbolism we often find many elements brought in that are essential and necessary elements from the standpoint of utility. A symbol often represents the correct way of doing things and has a distinct literal value of its own.

When we start to study the processes of thinking we find symbolism an essential language with which to work out the problem. All of these Mutras represent conditions of consciousness and represent the schools of philosophy that attain certain conditions of consciousness through realization. (Mutra, or hand posture, is a combination of ritual and symbol). If you will examine the symbolism of the art of antiquity you will find there is a great love on the part of ancient artists to deify the palms of the hand; the palm of the hand is a secret and sacred part of the body. In mysticism, an eye is placed in the palm of the hand; it is very important. According to the secret doctrine the palms of the hands are the focal points of cosmic rays, moving in the body; consequently it is necessary, under certain conditions, to close these circuits by bringing the thumbs together; all of these Mutras therefore have a utilitarian aspect - they act as aids to concentration.

****

In ritualism we find peoples portraying cosmic processes; mythologies are rituals in print. We have a second degree of symbolism. (The first degree would be the abstract principle symbolized by the God; then man used to represent the God does certain things representing the powers of the Deity). When the story is told we have mythology; instead of seeing it done, we read about it being done.

Besides this you have simple symbols as they are; representing phases of consciousness and of life. There are many kinds of symbols; word symbols; musical symbols. Anything that is tangible can be converted into the intangible principle.

These are the major divisions of symbolism; if you can thoroughly understand these principles it will help you to realize that through observation these various symbols can be discerned; through Discrimination the relative parts of these symbols can be studied and the relationship determined; and by Concentration it is possible to pierce through the form of the symbol and arrive at its innate or internal meaning. A philosopher must analyse

Lecture # 12

SYMBOLISM (cont'd)
NEO-PLATONISM

Manly P. Hall   6/10/1928

Unpublished Pages of "*The Secret Teachings of All Ages*"

LECTURES BY MANLY P. HALL　　　　　　　　　　　　　　　　　　　　　　　NO. 12

SYMBOLISM (Continued)
NEO-PLATONISM

　　　　The three divisions of simple symbolism are: the Allegory (the Dot); the Ritual (the Line) and the Material Object Symbol (the Circle). These systems are somewhat allied to the three spheres of consciousness, with the simple material object comprising the Force emblem; the ritual, the mental emblem and the allegory as the ethical or spiritual emblem.

　　　　Every object in the visible universe is an appropriate symbol of some invisible process or phase of existence. In our book we have brought out several phases of symbolism. Of course the symbol is closely related to the cipher. The cipher is the secret method of writing, and the language of symbols is akin to the language of cryptograms. From the early middle ages, down to the 19th century, systems of cipher writing were of very great importance. Then for a considerable period of time ciphers retired from prominence; only to return in the 20th century with great force, in two distinct lines of expression - (1) financial ciphers and (2) political or governmental ciphers. By the use of the cipher private transactions of institutions are not made known to the public. Governments have elaborate secret codes; some of them complicated - some quite simple. The use of codes in sending government information is very old; we find them in Egypt and in Greece. During the World War the art of cipher writing was elevated again to a position of importance. The book used by both the allies and the German forces during the war was probably the rarest work on cryptograms; it was published in 1600 (?) and had never been translated out of the Latin. This work was published by Sir Francis Bacon; the contents being the profoundest of occult philosophy. (The title page from this book is to be found in Mr. Hall's Book).

　　　　Nearly all of the ciphers of the middle ages have been made worthless by the law of recurrences. If you will take a chapter or a large sized page of a book, you will find that on every page of that book the letters will fail to a certain percentage; no matter what page there will be more 'E's' on that page than on any other; if you will count each letter on the page and find out how many there are, and put them down in the order of their recurrence, the letter that occurs most often is 'E'; the next is a certain other vowel. This law of recurrence has spoiled the ancients' system of ciphers, for the continued use of certain characters revealed the method.

　　　　From about 1400, down to the beginning of the 19th century, Europe passed through a period which may be called a truly 'Dark Age'; they were ages of intolerance - religious, political, scientific; the more that laws were passed to prevent man's thinking, the more certain he was to think. During those centuries there were a great many scientists; they were unusually privileged because thinkers were left completely alone, and were so isolated that they devoted years to the concentration of their study; they meditated on the mysteries of nature, and discovered many things we know nothing about today. These men, realizing that their discoveries were heresy, were marked men with a price on their heads; but they made every effort possible to perpetuate their discoveries. From the beginning of printing, in the 14th century, to the 19th century, their books concealed within the simple meaning a profound meaning.

　　　　At the same period - between 1405 and 1750, there also appeared a profound effort to reconstruct pagan philosophy. People had become excited about the real meaning of the Scriptures and began to investigate the philosophy and ethics; the result was that the books of the middle ages contained profound allusions to the material of ancient ethics. The methods of marking these books were manifold; the most common way of marking them was on the title page (by use of heraldic devices, etc); and by means of tail-pieces to chapters. In symbolism we have a key to the method of deciphering the material hidden by cryptograms; this is a division of symbolism which is a whole subject in itself.

Besides these matters we want to call your attention to: (1) the art of the ancient world is practically totally symbolic. Almost every figure carved had a double meaning. (2) No single science has contributed as much to symbolism as mathematics. Because of the exactness of mathematics (if the numbers are chosen with proper care) they can be worked into a science of relationship that will carry a wealth of symbolic meaning. Symbols used to convey the idea of relationships are often based on mathematics; one of the most fundamental symbols is the 47th proposition of Euclid: (attributed to Euclid but brought by Pythagoras from Egypt). To this day the mysteries of the Platonic solids remain unsolved; the making of these solids is one of the most involved processes man can undertake; the mind, in attempting to formulate and visualize the parts of these bodies, receives a peculiar expansion no other method can possibly induce. Pythagoras was the great master of the use of mathematics in symbolism. Numbers themselves are innately symbolic. We have for many centuries concerned ourselves with the outer meaning of things; we are attempting to dominate the outer nature of everything, but know nothing concerning the inner nature of anything; we are, therefore, supremely ignorant.

Besides mathematics, we come to a second division of the symbolic language; that is the language of color. Color symbolism is the most valuable form we now have. Color therapy is recognized as a legitimate method of the art of healing; the influence of color is very profound. Colors are very vital in the life of the individual; and the colors with which we surround ourselves have a profound effect on our attitudes towards existence. Students of culture and aesthetics are beginning to concern themselves with the meaning of color tones; we begin to realize that color has a life in it; color is an expression or medium of moods – each tone equivalent to a human mood, and as color is appropriate to symbolize moods, so color will also induce moods. Color is a wonderful power, and as we evolve higher in our consciousness of color we begin to depart from the brilliant tones and pass into the pastel tones; we will have a greater interest in the more delicate tones and sounds. Every color has its sound; every sound has its color.

In symbolism music has great power; music, like color, is used to symbolize moods. It also has a therapeutic value. The thing used to symbolize a state, is capable of producing the state it symbolizes. It is usually chosen with the thought in mind that it will stimulate the attitude or condition in the one gazing at it. Color and sound in healing (sound in the sense of the mantra and chant, as well as music) – these are problems of harmonics.

In the study of astronomy you must realize that it was used as a method of symbolism and was allegorical, and should not be interpreted in its physical sense. They symbolized certain principles by the sun, moon and starts.

****

From this point we wish to turn to an important division of symbolism that arose in the middle ages – the problem of the Kabala. The Kabala is, technically, the Israel revolt against literalism. Those who have been ahead of the rest have always realized the greatest enemy of humankind is the literal mind. In the Kabala we find a supreme effort on the part of the ancient Jewish philosophers to keep alive the body of the Jewish law. They realized the same thing Christianity is now realizing – that somewhere along the line they had lost the Spirit of their doctrine. There are many meanings to the word 'Spirit'; spirit of a thing is concerned with the inner life of the thing itself;

the spirit is the secret doctrine, and whenever a faith loses contact with its secret doctrine it is said to have 'lost its spirit'. The secret doctrine is that higher and more technical knowledge which explains the reason for the other or outer knowledge. The spirit remained as a tenacious clinging power, holding the race together; with the idealism dead, the physical power of the race decayed. The 'letter' of a thing is always cold.

During the first and second centuries, A.D., the realization of the death of the spirit in the secret teachings of the preceding ages was very apparent. Many scholars realized they had nothing but empty shells; no one knew the 'whys' of anything. There arose a school of magnificent thinkers - namely, the Neo-Platonists. They are generally presumed to have been revivalists of Platonism, but they were not - they had a totally new attitude on knowledge, and it was this attitude that saved the secret doctrine from entirely disappearing. It was not a localized movement; it existed in Syria, Greece, Rome, Egpyt, etc - it existed in several countries simultaneously. It was the supreme effort of the wise to preserve the secret doctrine - to reenliven the letter of the law. We have several great institutions; (1) the theory of Mysticism. In the ancient Greek Mysteries there were two degrees; the first degree was the Mystic (one who sees through a mist - generally applied now to all who seek to establish a metaphysical basis of existence) one opposed to the theory of literalism.) The Mystic is one who attempts to establish the superphysical basis of existence, whereas the materialist seeks to establish the physical basis. Mysticism can be traced from the Platonists; the sum and the value of Neo-Platonism lay in its secret teaching. That teaching is a key to our whole theory of symbolism.

The Neo-Platonists, including Jew, Christian, and pagans - postulated first of all one knowledge - knowledge being the sum of reality, and Wisdom the knowledge of reality. He who knows that which is real, is wise; he only who knows that which is real is capable of discriminating between reality and illusion. That in all the things in which knowledge exists there is unity; and any man once learning a fact will know the same thing any other man knows who has learned that thing. The existence of one doctrine —claiming that when man reaches truth they all come to a point of agreement; where is disagreement is a lack of knowledge. The Neo-Platonists moved from that hypothesis that all religions and philosophies had their foundation in knowledge, and that while they were in their pure state were one with the nature of truth. But that through the inability of man - as a partly evolved creature - to comprehend or recognize truth, the divine realities of these various doctrine became enmeshed in illusion; wisdom disappeared and only the shell remained. The Neo-Platonist presumed there was one religion; this one religion was one with philosophy; that there was but one philosophy in the world and it was one with religion; since religion and philosophy are one knowledge, there never has been but one philosophy in the world; there never has been but one religion in the world; there never has been but one science in the world. These three are the phases of one Truth, and there can never be but one Truth in the Universe. This was the great foundation of the Neo-Platonists - an enormous concept. This was the first supreme tenet of Neo-Platonism.

Its second great contribution to thinking was something it would do the modern scientific world good to get hold of. The Neo-Platonist says the only way that man can ever reach reality is by means of the unfoldment of himself. That no religion, no philosophy, no art or science can make him any better than his own acts; they are simply designed to show him how to do better, but not to take the place of the doing. They do not actually do anything for man; they simply show man what to do for himself. Neo-Platonism says that as consciousness of man unfolds his knowledge increases; consequently the Neo-Platonist assumed that within man's own constitution was a mass of scientific equipment, a mass of spiritual equipment - and if man would concentrate on the unfoldment of his own powers he would reach knowledge. Neo-Platonism declared the path to wisdom lay inward - not outward. Neo-Platonism was a fourth dimensional journey, and the path to Self was inward to cause. They presumed, and proved very well, that their teaching was actually a revelation of the process of the unfolding of Self. That the object of every religion was Man; and the subject the unfoldment of man's powers. Neo-Platonism was hated by the literalists; it doomed dogma; it reduced words to a minimum and put the emphasis on deeds.

The school of the Kabala discovered the secret doctrine of Israel, and tried to demonstrate that the doctrine of Israel were spiritual revelations and not physical laws. Concealed within the doctrine of Israel was a secret doctrine concerning the method of human regeneration - viz., the method of lifting man from the state of comparative ignorance to a state of absolute knowing. The secret doctrine conceals under many a manifold veil, the philosophy of human completion; every one is concerned with the same thing - the regeneration of man and the unfoldment of the latent potentialities within. In every religion, east and west, there are many speculations; but the secret doctrine is an operative mysticism by which man, as a physical being, is united with his own spiritual nature.

Neo-Platonism gave to the world the following: all religions, sciences and philosophies have, as their purpose, the unfoldment of man. The physical body of humanity is preserved by the physical law - the physical law is to regulate the physical life of man. Behind this is the spiritual law, to regulate the spiritual living of the individual; by the regulation of spiritual living the consciousness is increased in power; man is capable of forcing the growth of his conscious faculties. The modern world is ready to believe you can 'Burbank' a potato - but not the human mind. The whole structure of philosophy is based on the hypothesis that you can force the faculties; that you can develop them beyond a normal state by a certain set process of culture. They gave man certain things to do; they caused certain activities to take place in him; they caused him to create environments which drew out conditions within himself. They could take a brain and build it by forced culture to correspond to a brain two or three hundred years ahead of its time - it would think in the same terms as other minds would that had passed through the natural growth. The Mysteries found the way of producing the effect of diminishing time; instead of taking 1000 years to produce an effect, they could produce it in a few years, by formulae; whoever has a brain greater than his world, controls his world. But a mind 2000 years ahead of his race endangers his race; the power of that mind is enormous because its clarity of function exceeds others of its time. For thousands of years these bands of initiated minds investigated the process of culturing the human plant. This secret knowledge of how to build and unfold consciousness was the major part of their secret doctrine; this was the thing they were not permitted to commit to writing; which they would not entrust to those who did not take the same vows they did; they could not be sure of the moral fineness of the temperament. They could force the growth of certain parts; they could not be certain all parts would grow together. There were tests of character by means of which they tested the individual as to his fitness to receive a mental stimulus; if he proved fitted to receive this growth and would be capable of using it wisely, then he was turned over to the priests and the cultural stimulus was given.

The secret doctrine is always in symbol. When it became necessary to communicate these things they were concealed in the symbol and the symbol corresponded to the initiation process; those who cannot now see through the intricacies of the symbol is not ready for the initiation: the symbol is the custodian of the doctrine. If the modern mystic fails to comprehend the symbol itn proves that he has not yet an understanding, sufficiently great to use them rightly and is thus rejected from the temple by his inability to understand the symbol.

****

Lecture # 13

SYMBOLISM (cont'd)
THE QUATERNARY

Manly P. Hall   6/11/1928

Unpublished Pages of "*The Secret Teachings of All Ages*"

LECTURES BY MANLY P. HALL   NO. 13

SYMBOLISM (Continued)

THE QUATERNARY

From the symbolism of the triangle we shall not turn to the symbolism of the square - the four-sided geometrical figure which represents the inferior or lower nature of the universe, and, by analogy, the inferior or lower nature of the individual. As the 3 is the symbol of spiritual activity, so the 4 is the emblem of form; it is the symbol of the substance worked upon; the universe is therefore, in manifestation, symbolized by the 7; consisting of a three-fold spiritual causal part, and a four-fold material or effectual part. Many symbols are used to represent the four-fold material part; the number system, from which this symbolism is derived, has its origin in the symbolism of Pythagoras, who used the One - or the Dot - as the symbol of the human monad, or cause of things; the Two they called the Line because the line has two ends; the Three was the simplest of the enclosing forms, therefore the triangle was the simplest of 'fences' in which you can limit an area. You can also encircle it, but whereas the circle is apparently a single line it is considered the most intricate of all figures inasmuch as it is made up of a number of infinitely minute lines. The simplest figure is the triangle - the number 3; the simplest figure that can enclose completely an area is the tetrahedron, the four-faced solid.

You have all heard the familiar expression, 'the four corners of the earth'. There is nothing in the universe, cosmically speaking, that has corners; the universe is nothing but spheres; the higher we go we find manifestation in the form of spheres.

The square as the emblem of matter, brings with it a great many interesting considerations. First of all, the ancients considered all matter to be composed of four primordial elements; these elements were called earth, fire, air and water. They believed the physical universe consisted of the four primordial elements and consequently they came to personalize these elements and consider them as deities who controlled the various parts of nature.

If you come forward into the modern thought you will find this substantiated; protoplasm is presumed to be the basis of form and it is composed of four principles; hydrogen, oxygen, nitrogen and carbon - again the four elements of the ancients. The cross, like the square, is the symbol of these four elements; also the four spheres or planes of consciousness. The cross is reduced, from the cosmic symbol of redemption, to the natural emblem of the earth; among almost every nation the earth has a symbol that is either a square or a cross. You can reduce the idea still further and discover the cross to be the emblem of material power. If you will look closely at a crucifix you will find the form of the body upon it is the form of an inverted triangle (the feet the lower part of the triangle). The black cross represents the four-fold physical constitution while the body upon it is the Christ (three-fold spiritual constitution) - Spirit crucified upon matter. The cross is the proper symbol of the Fallen Man - life imprisoned in matter.

The Greeks posited a fifth element; the Akasha, above and permeating the other four elements. This fifth element is the 'ether' of the scientists, but of which they cannot prove its existence. The four elements, in conditions of increasing dignity, represent qualities and characteristics.

Brahma is to the Hindoo mysticism what the Grand Man is to the Jewish symbolism; it represents the structure of world form, and is generally presumed to be the Father Spirit. Out of the various parts of Brahma issue the four castes which are the basis of the Hindu sociological system. The Brahman priests became literalists and paralyzed India with the caste system, which should have illuminated them. Brahma was born with wisdom, the Master of all men; born with a peculiar dignity, foreordained to rule the world; he was the Mind-Born Son of the World. Out of the red shoulders the Red Men - the Warrior Class came (Buddha); out of the body of Brahman, the Brown Men came, the shopkeepers - the craftsmen - whose duty it was to defend the Brahman; to serve and supply his needs; out of the feet of the Brahman issued the slaves - the abject servant of Brahman. Brahman's symbol is air; the Warrior - Fire; the Shopkeeper - Water; and the physical Earth - the slave or servant. Fire, Water and earth were fashioned to serve Air:

```
                    Air (Mind)   *
                              *  *
         Warrior (Fire)    *       *  Shopkeeper (Water)
                              *  *
                                *
                     Sudra (Earth)
```

The four castes became emblematic of the four states of consciousness; also the symbols of dimension. (1) Air signified the Mind (highest of the 4 bodies of man's personal nature)
(Warriors):   (2) Emotion signified the basis of sense powers; defense of the mind is placed in the hands of the emotions, which are to be transmuted)
(Shopkeeper): (3) Generation, the power of growth; represents the vital temperament. (Craftsmen necessary to the reconstruction of vital energy; protect and keep perfect the 'House of Brahma').
(Sudra):   (4) The physical body (servant) would disintegrate unless kept by the three higher elements.

Man, as a 3-fold spiritual nature: (Creative Spirit   (Father)
                                     (Perpetuating Spirit   (Mother)
                                     (Incarnating Physical Spirit (Son)

Man's four vehicles, or garments: (Mental body
                                     (Emotional body
                                     (Vital body
                                     (Physical body

* * * * * *

We now turn to the symbol of the Cherubim of Ezekiel; the four elements of the inferior nature; the One Body with the Four Heads; the four heads represent the origin or soul seats of the four parts of the material nature; out of the spiritual nature, with its three parts, is exuded the quaternary of material constitution: Bull (Earth) Eagle (Water) Lion (Fire) Man's Head (Air). These powers are presumed to have their seats in the pole centers of the various natures in man; the physical or elemental body has its seat in the heart (head of the Bull); the Eagle in the spleen; the Lion in the liver; Man in the Brain. By means of a vast number of mechanisms these four great centers of form-building power eject into the physical body of man their streams that maintain the balance of the physical body; they control, as personalized deities, but actually as principles, the spiritual potentialities.

Another point: (How the universe builds form). These centers are generally represented as flowers; the flower is always the symbol of two things - the generative process or else the blossoms of electric force. These centers of power are the basis - the germs of man's fourfold personal nature; these are again analogous to the acorn; they are seed pods, and, like seed pods, contain an infinite number of potential germs; it is from these seeds the various bodies grow. The mind body of man grows from a single primitive cell; the substance which does the thinking is what grows; mental protoplasm from which ideas develop.

Mind is not spirit, but Substance - substance of thinking: the minute atom composing this substance is called by Herbert Spencer the 'Mentoid'. These seeds themselves are preserved in the seed pod; these pods are not composed of the substance of any one of the bodies (mental, emotional, vital, etc) but the seeds are capable of attracting to them the essences and elements that will build bodies. We have, therefore, four seed pods, transubstantial; invisible, intangible - but an essential part of our constitution. When we begin the process of building bodies we build by objectifying these seeds in a concatanated order - the mental (air); the emotional body (fire); the vital body (water); and the physical or earth body.

When disintegration takes place it means the reverse order; the pods cut off their communication with the body; when the root is removed all the branches die. After a certain period of manifestation these germs retire; the body then disintegrates (Death). A necessary point; each one of these seedpods, from which is objectified a body, is composed of the substance of spirit; consequently possessing consciousness. These pods become the depositories of the records of the life of each of these bodies; these records, being accepted into the substance of the pods, are the basis of the attitudes and peculiarities of the next tree to grow out of them; the new germ, with the new body, coming into expression, is molded and influenced by the characteristics and traits of the earlier pods; heredity is consciousness seeking an environment consistent with its own seed centers.

* * * * * * *

Realizing the number 3 to be the symbol of cosmic urge, we find the 4 to be the symbol of natural resistance, or the emblem of the Adversary - the thing which resists the impulse to accomplishment. This limiting influence becomes emblematic of the prison of form, the inhibiting nature of crystallized matter. Crystallization (Water) and Vitalization (Fire) are the two forces in nature ever struggling against each other. Fire represents spirit; water represents matter. Out of the blend of the material elements of matter and the spiritual agents of life there is established a middle ground, which is organized matter - the organic matter; also, in its higher form, highly organized constitution in which matter and activity are blended in the organization of a functioning unit. The perfect man represents a perfectly harmonious blending of these two parts.

* * * * * * *

Lecture # 14

RELATIONSHIP EXISTING BETWEEN SUBSTANCE OF MIND AND SUBSTANCE OF SPIRIT

Manly P. Hall   6/12/1928

Unpublished Pages of "*The Secret Teachings of All Ages*"

LECTURES BY MANLY P. HALL   NO. 14

RELATIONSHIP EXISTING BETWEEN SUBSTANCE OF MIND
AND SUBSTANCE OF SPIRIT

An individual to whom a fact is literally revealed concerning some subject of importance is cheated of the privilege of having discovered that fact for himself. That which we are told stimulates only the memory. The mind, like the body, must be exercised and if properly exercised gains strength with activity. The more we depend upon the wise the weaker we become ourselves; the more we depend upon ourselves the more we become like the wise. Wisdom is the result of a personal growth.

The symbol occupies a most important position, in the fact that it does not tell you enough, to do your thinking for you; it just tells you enough to intrigue you. It is necessary to think about the symbol, and try to visualize what it stands for; it is necessary to approach it with every bit of mental alertness the individual possesses. Symbolism is a language which encourages creative thinking in that it encourages the mind to dare something; if the individual starts to think he is naturally going to establish standards of right and wrong; he is going to recognize new elements in life - and every individual fundamentally knows that true thinking is the deadly enemy of selfishness.

Symbolism, unknown to the person working with it, is a continual mental stimulus; it awakens the most powerful of faculties - outside the memory - curiosity. The mind becomes involved in the desire to find out what the symbol stands for; it calls up size and proportion, form, observation, reflection, discrimination, individuality, etc. These faculties begin to relate and correlate; the symbol is related to something that is known, and the mind tries to work out the philosophical reason for the symbol; the mind is tantalized into action by the presence of something it wants to know. This process results in a direct mental unfoldment; gradually the mind becomes accustomed to a new concept - looking through the nature of things; it begins to see symbols in everything. After a certain length of time in this type of endeavor the mind takes on the power of grasping the meaning of things. This is a real thinking process.

A symbol is best worked out alone; the most perfect conclusions come as a result of direct concentration; symbols are intended to centralize faculties, and to understand any symbol in its completeness it is necessary to draw all the faculties upon it. By this concentration thoughts are born - realizations come into expression and the mind begins to work out things all by itself. This is the most important form of thinking and is encouraged by symbolism. The individual who is studying the symbol objectifies into it his own consciousness; therefore the symbol he interprets becomes the emblem of his own power of interpretation. The symbol becomes a mirror in which the symbolist sees his own knowledge reflected back at him; he attributes to the symbol his own condition of thinking.

The symbol, if designed correctly by its original designer (and most of the ancient symbols were) is also, to a certain degree, capable of giving out thoughts; the symbol itself is more or less alive; it has a certain radiating power - and aside from the interpretations given to the symbol it also is capable of giving its own. To draw out of the symbol what it means is the result of an analysis of the parts of the emblem itself; it is the result of a power to grasp and correlate all of its parts. It is easier to put interpretations on to a symbol than to draw them out of the symbol itself.

There is a certain amount of 'mental purging' necessary before one can 'build the temple'. The clearing away of the debris of Opinion is one of the first steps towards the development of the philosophic mind. These various adversaries are many; most people are broadminded on everything except one or two pet fancies. Pythagoras attacked these inconsistencies and tried to drive them out, because he realized that until these notions are gone thinking cannot begin. To think honestly requires a certain mysterious attitude towards life. Each individual can be his own taskmaster and do the necessary chastising that will insure the rationality of his own mind. We must learn to rule our own faculties. There are two phases of the past; the heroic and the mediocre. The ladder we rise upon is the ladder of the heroic past; we must differentiate between these two divisions of the ages gone.

Symbolism is a great help in our quest of new attitudes. It puts us, temporarily, en rapport with our own tomorrows. Things that lie latent in us become, for the moment, active; we attune ourselves to the greatness of the tomorrow; we are, temporarily, greater than we are today. It is this creative mind - creative imagining - that induces growth. The philosopher lives completely in tomorrows - it might be better to say he annihilates the idea of time; he lives in the eternal expanse of duration.

Time is something we have created ourselves; time is our own method of estimating duration. We have taken eternity - the limitless - and made it limited. We have created terms designating the infinite multiplicity of change. There is no line whatsoever between the past, the present and the future. Instead of seeing existence divided into periods of time, the philosopher sees it as conditions of consciousness. He divides it into states of being; and time as a process of measuring the flight of eternity is eliminated. Time is but a hypothetical thing; duration exists and is the infinite period of all things; it is just long enough to be completely sufficient for the perfection of everything.

We have in philosophy the slow but sure plodding towards accomplishment. Time is the interval between the extreme opposites of accomplishment; time will never give out until accomplishment is complete, because time hangs on accomplishment as a dependency. While anything can go from one condition to another the field of duration will surround that activity, and consequently it will be presumed to take place 'in time'.

Before philosophy can come the mind must be cleared of the accumulations of false thinking. When it is free and becomes a clean mind it has then a certain power - a certain grasp. It has a certain naive quality most important to it; a simplicity, a kindliness; a certain indication that the cargo of undesirables has gone overboard. There is always - where you find the philosophic best - a certain simplicity which means that the mind has discarded things of no importance; the mind grasps the kernel of the proposition and lets the fancies go. This is the point of 'understanding'. The most rigid mental discipline must be gone through to cleanse the mind of its tendencies.

Philosophy is almost always not only a molder of mental qualities but these mental qualities continually come outward and mold the objectified physical nature. There is a certain 'appearance' in the face; a certain childlike expression of joy - sincerity that is a clear indication of the quality underneath. It is so powerful that it reaches beyond the individual; it will add a certain aura of loveableness; a certain appeal to the nature. Thinking increases the observational faculties, the reflective faculties; it broadens the humanitarian faculties; it brings with it a very magnificent understanding; and, more wonderful, the tolerance or understanding that does not need excuses. The reward of philosophy is that understanding that makes the world seem good; we cannot live in the world of good until we find it, and we do not find it until we know what Good is, and only by philosophy can we discover those fundamentals that enable us to see the greatness of Beauty and Goodness that permeate all existence.

Lecture # 15

ESOTERICISM AND EXOTERICISM

Manly P. Hall   6/13/1928

Unpublished Pages of "*The Secret Teachings of All Ages*"

LECTURES BY MANLY P. HALL   NO. 15
                                                             6/13/28

ESOTERICISM AND EXOTERICISM

In the ancient mysteries wisdom knowledge was divided into two general parts or sections; that which was called the exoteric and that which was called the esoteric knowledge. 'Exoteric' may be literally interpreted to signify 'revealed law' - no matter how great a secret may be, the moment it becomes revealed it becomes the property of all This does not of course necessarily mean that all will understand; but the bans are removed from some form of knowledge and it is given to the world to do with as the world may see fi' The whole structure of science, philosophy, theology, etc - as it is known to the world - is the exoteric structure. In each succeeding generation the natural growth of humanity results in the human mind's increasing capacity to understand, and as the mind grows in the power of understanding certain parts of the hidden law are revealed - for the law is revealed as rapidly as human consciousness evolves to the point where it can use the law intelligently. The problems and mysteries of the ancients - which were only discussed in the depths of the sanctuary - are now within the reach of the child; the ban of secrecy has been lifted, and as time goes on this ban will be continually lifted, revealing more and more of knowledge.

The word 'esoteric' signifies the unrevealed doctrine; it is that part of the law that has never come into the possession of the race; it hasnever been deposited in humanity but remains deposited only inthe elect. It is that part of the law that cannot be secured without fulfilling the requirements of the Masters - the keepers of the esoteric law. It is a philosophy communicated by the master to the disciple - from mouth to ear. (The only book ever written concerning the secret doctrine is The Anthropos - written in Greek and buried in a crypt; unavailable to man). Books have been written presumably dealing with this subject, but in every case they are books of hints; they point, but they never show the thing pointed at. If you can read between the lines you may read something; the ability to read between the lines is a developed faculty. If you have that faculty - of piercing literal statements - you will find these books contain a hidden law but it remains esoteric in that no word of it is actually on the written page. The use of the allegory and myth are but convenient methods of saying things without saying them. Leaving it to the reader to read what is not said, and understand what is not set forth; this is the height of mental culture.

The esoteric law underlies the body of knowledge; it is the invisible, intangible part concerning which there is an infinite amount of speculation. The esoteric philosophy, like spiritual consciousness, may be briefly divided into three parts; the dot, the line and the circle; but for the sake of a simple series of terms suppose we call one of these phases the Eastern School, another the Western School, and between the two, a school that is a blending of both. The secret doctrine, in eastern philosophy, is purely concerned with the development or release of consciousness from the state of consciousness and its absolute absorption into the nature of Absolute Being. The Western School, however, moves from a different angle; it is concerned with the building up of super-individuality, whereas the Eastern School is concerned with the annihilation of individuality. The Middle School approaches the subject with the positive Western and the abstract and abstruse eastern culture, blending them and partaking of both. These schools have never appeared publicly as systems of philosophy; but an infinite number of systems of philosophy have been given to the world by individual members of these schools. All the systems revealed are allegorical; they are blinds - which is the only way the teachings can be given the world. The nature and construction of the Center itself is infinitely abstruse.

India's secret doctrine is her priceless heritage; it is her unwritten law. It is something hidden, to which the yearning minds of Indian students aspire. Through a multitude of methods of preparation they seek to find - that is, to receive the inner teaching. There - as here - the secret law is not revealed to the multitude; it is essentially the mastery of the processes whereby the Godhood of man is accomplished; and it is not good that this be revealed.

The body of the ancient wisdom is a thoroughly organized body; it is a pulsating organism of power - far more powerful than we know anything about in our world of force. The secret schools were not destroyed; they are totally beyond the ability of material power to destroy. With its finely constructed method, it has always existed and always will exist, and it must continually be conserved - not only for the safety of the race, but for the protection of its own arcana. The work of the ancient wisdom, however, does not show as much as people might presume it should. The purpose of wisdom is not to interfere with the working of mankind; it is to insure that mankind does not destroy itself. The secret doctrine is not supposed to take the place of living; its great purpose is to help each mind to unfold itself.

We find the ancient school retiring into the recesses of unknown lands; concealed in a way that it can never be discovered. It works and controls as it sees fit. It continually brings into its own body certain illuminated men and women who have elevated themselves to the point where they become necessary. The purpose of human accomplishment is not necessarily an initiation into these bodies; those who enter do so for a peculiar purpose; they are those who are fitted to become teachers; this secret school is a band of servants; they become θ so to speak - the elder brothers of humanity - a group that steps to one side in the service of their fellows.

The thing we want to bring to your mind is this; if you are interested in the secret doctrine - if you desire to possess the esoteric knowledge - it is absolutely essential that you develop discrimination to the point where it prevents you from confusing issues; that you will be saved from the pitfalls of false knowledge; subject everything to a very careful analysis, and employ discrimination.

****

REMARKS ON MR. HALL'S BOOK

When you start reading the book we do not want you to approach it with any illusions - any misconceptions of its contents. It is called an Encyclopedia; it is an Encyclopedia of symbols. More than simply symbols, it is an effort to begin an interpretation of these symbols. It is not intended to be a creation that claims any merit from the standpoint that it is new or unusual.

The book is not esoteric; it is simply a reconstruction of the gateways of ancient learning; it is the Front Door - nothing more. It does not tell you very much; it is simply that path leading up to ancient wisdom. You will find in it 45 chapters - all presumably different - and yet all exactly the same; it may be some time before you notice the repetitions; 45 chapters tell one story and repeat it again and again and again. But each chapter repeats it in a different way - reaching a different type of mind. The book is simply a guide in direction; a book on the subject of these teachings cannot, and never has, and never will, reveal the teaching; but if you are willing to take it and work with it conscientiously, we believe you will derive from it material which will help you to reconstruct what is not there - to see what is not written - to discover what is not on the page itself.

We have spent a great deal of time in the archives of ancient philosophy trying to discover the order and sequence of these different mysteries; we have found on every hand one cry going up: 'This is a most interesting subject but unfortunately there isn't anything known about it - there is no information available.' We have worked very hard to find the scraps that could be discovered and have sought to piece them together according to their own nature; therefore do not be surprised if you find apparent contradictions on every page - there is no effort made to make the different systems conform - it is more valuable that they be <u>as they are</u>. The information is presented, as far as possible, in the spirit of the original writing. It is not what you are going to get by reading this book that will help you; it is what you will get if you will think about what you read. Read it alone - by yourself; the first step to knowing is independence.

We believe the pointers in this book will assist you to reconstruct the body of world learning; it is only the individual who does the work that gets ahead - the power to do things. This is the very kernel - the basis of philosophy, because philosophy is simply knowledge, and knowledge comes from a certain activity that is necessary in order to understand.

Accident and design have conspired to delay this book, and to make it as difficult as possible. This book is built and prepared - as far as we could do it - in the same style that the ancients gave their knowledge to the world; it is built and presented in a style appropriate to the subject matter; it is as beautiful as the printer's craft can make it; everything that goes into the making of it is as beautiful as could be secured; we have verified, checked and rechecked everything in the book; the material is literally true. The important thing will be to reconstruct out of the book one thought; it is written around one thought - and the discovery of that one thought is the supreme achievement in reading the book. The material there represents one end of an endless thread that winds out in all parts of creation - as long as space is broad, and as deep as the profundities of the Abyss.

The book is like unto a door - a gate, in some old sanctuary, containing within it a wealth of imagery; a wealth of mysteries, designs and figures. When you have wandered therein you might say to yourself: 'I wish I had a guide to tell me what these things mean'. And you will find your guide to be your own rational soul.

****

Lecture # 16

NUMBERS

Manly P. Hall   6/14/1928

Unpublished Pages of "*The Secret Teachings of All Ages*"

LECTURES BY MANLY P. HALL

NO. 16
6/14/28

NUMBERS

We find numbers a very important key to ancient thinking. Without the assistance of numbers it is impossible to find what the names of the gods stand for. We find nearly all of the names of the great gods of antiquity contain seven letters; this 'seven' is very important. Serapis is sometimes called the 'Seven-letter God' - the letters indicating seven rays of power. If you will take the names of the various gods of the Greek pantheon you will find each one is a cunningly concealed numerical cryptogram. The number itself a key to the potency under consideration. The names of the gods should never be translated - the value of the word is destroyed. You should also realize that the vowels are related to cosmic activities; they are the Seven Spirits before the Throne.

If you will close your eyes and keep very quiet and think the letters of the alphabet - one after another - you will discover it is necessary to think of these letters in different places; some as inside of you - others you must think of as outside you; some above, some as below; the process of thinking of them projects the consciousness of them into different places or parts.

Another point; numbers and letters are all of them peculiarly formed; the physical form of them is significant. They are certain combinations of lines and points. In the Hebrew all letters are composed of a certain number of Yods put together. It is a secret symbol (the Yod) - the germ or seed of life. The letters of the Hebrew alphabet are very carefully shaped; there are several divisions of letters - some are gutterals, others pronounced on the teeth; the Hebrews have placed their letters into groups according to the way they are formed in the mouth. In many languages it is necessary to lift the tongue against the roof of the mouth in speaking of deities; the tongue is raised in adoration of the Lord.

By means of numbers we are able to get at the meaning concealed in words; according to the methods of numerology all numbers have to be reduced to numbers under 10. I have checked over carefully the two systems (ancient and modern) and in no case have the two given the same results; it stands to reason that one cannot be exactly right. We will advise you to discard the modern, and go back to the ancient system. You will find that the science of numbers consists of something very important; it can be elevated and become an abstract science; you will not require outside help to work it out if you will observe the law of recurrences. (See Pythagorean methods).

All numbers are combinations of the first 10; the first 10 are manifestations of the First One. The One means the All; it is the number to which all other numbers can be reduced; it is the beginning; it is the sum of all numbers; the One is always the symbol of the Supreme Power; it is the unit of all things - everything made up of an infinite number of Ones. The One is the seed.

As One is the supreme power of activity, so Two is the passive agent of nature - Isis, the Great Mother; it is the symbol of the first separation; the Two represents the beginning of diversity. The One is the state of supreme wisdom; the Two is supreme ignorance (ignorance where is belief in good and evil. Buddha said: 'That is impossible, because if Good cannot control evil then it is not the Supreme Good, and if Good does not control evil, still it is not the Supreme Good".) These are human attitudes, and in no way does the concept of good and evil have any effect on the things themselves; they are illusions of the human mind. (Illustration - the tomato).

The Three was accepted by the Pythagoreans as the first real number. One and Two were abstract principles; the three was organized consciousness; it was the 'spirit' with its three phases. All spiritual activity naturally moves in three lines - three primitive manifestations. The three was the symbol of the Trinity - the First Outpouring from the One; the One which gives birth to the three out of Itself - forms the Fourth (the receptacle).

The Fourth - the symbol of matter; organized universe of form. The Four was considered by the ancients as a spiritual number - the symbol of the Demiurgus; in astronomy the sign of Jupiter. (Jehovah; it represents the Son, the Lord of the World).

The Five - ancient Pythagorean symbol of healing. The Five, of course, has always been the symbol of magic. It is a very interesting emblem and one containing a great many powers. It is the symbol of ether: (the 4 represents the elements; the 5th element is Ether). It is the natural symbol of Man; the five senses; it is emblematic of liberation - the attainment of human perfection. The pentagram (5-pointed star) if inverted, becomes the symbol of black magic. (All symbols come as a result of very profound study of natural law; they must be symmetrical. There are 72 names of God and there are 72 degrees between the points of the pentagram. The proper use of these symbols is by a fundamental knowledge. Paracelsus said a thing which is drawn is alive; and a word written on paper is just as much alive as a spoken word. Our thoughts are alive; our acts, our words. These symbols are, therefore, emblematic of certain positive energies, and there is a profound science in the preparation of them. Wherever these symbols or doctrines fall into the hands of perverted minds who use them for selfish purposes the power of the emblem itself steps in; no one who uses the symbols of white magic can use the symbols of black magic; and no one who uses the perverted forms can use the symbols of white magic. An individual who wishes to do an evil deed and cloak it in a good deed, finds himself bitten by the symbol itself; there is always something done to them to destroy the potency of their original purpose. When this happens you will find there are no longer 72 points to the pentagram; a distorted symbol always signifies the wrong use of the symbol. Black magic is nothing but a shadow; it is impossible for any living thing to cast a perfect shadow of itself. There is no substance in the world of shadows. (The Devil is God, inverted. - Kabalistic statement)

The Six is the interlaced triangle; the Shield of David. This is the number of equilibrium; in Six we have consciousness and form together; at a proper balance. It is the symbol of human consciousness because it represents balance of spirit and matter. The Six Days of Labor - the creative period of consciousness; the symbol of the power which must unfold itself in the perfection of man. It is a royal symbol; the symbol of attainment.

The Seven is the most famous, the most powerful of all numbers. The Seven is the key to the vowels; the seven vowels of the Sacred Name. It is the symbol of the Law because it is the symbol of the Seven Governors of the World. It is the symbol of Force; the vital organs; the seven openings of the human head; the seven outer schools of the ancient wisdom; the seven periods of life - or seven ages of man, controlled by the seven planets in their proper order (infancy, the Moon; maturity, the Sun, etc); the completely awakened/senses will ultimately represent the jewels of consciousness in man.
seven

The Eight is called by the Greeks the Little Holy Number; it is the symbol representing the currents which connect the three centers of consciousness in God, Man and the Universe; the symbol of the serpent fire moving in the body, connecting the three centers - the heart, the head and the generative system. The Eight is a number made up of combinations of other numbers (in the study of numbers all the possible combinations represent various phases and powers of the number itself). Tones and half-tones of the octaves.

The Nine is the symbol of generation; it is one of the most important numbers in symbolism. The earth, the seven planets and the fixed stars equal 9, and represent the conditions of the soul or consciousness in the process of coming into manifestation. Life becomes involved in nine stages of preparation and man passes through a prenatal epoch into physical birth; there is also a philosophic preparation consisting of ascending nine steps of consciousness. (See chapter on Hermes).

As the Nine represents the process of spiritual and physical generation and regeneration, the Ten is the proper emblem of the completeness of the work. It is the symbol of the Universe. We have a chain of ten parts, leading up from the earth to the presence of the Deity; the Ten represents the whole creative and created systems.

****

Beginning with man's physical body: the physical form is composed of four elements - a square; outside of this is the square or power which corresponds to the Moon; outside this the cyclic poles of the planets; (physical body likened to the earth; vital body to the Moon, etc). After he reaches the 8th body outward (sphere of Saturn, which represents the extreme of his organized consciousness) there is the cycle of the 9th and 10th worlds; the auras or auric bodies work outward until every individual is surrounded by a globe or transparent egg. The Ptolemaic system is a complete cross section of the auric bodies of man himself.

Man studies the universe outside himself in order that he may understand the universe inside himself. The planets, constellations and the zodiac are all in you; the incarnating spiritual nature of man actually does come from the 9th sphere; these seed germs - if seen by superphysical means - the auric belt in the human body becomes visible as a mass of star-points (the Milky Way); this is the sphere that corresponds to the Milky Way in the universe.

The rising of man through the nine stages means that which is caused by the ascent of consciousness through the layers of his own nature, until the 10th sphere - which is Absolute Nature. He then finds himself en rapport with the nature of Absolute Being; he rises through these levels - the orbits of his own consciousness; If you will place the physical nature in the center you will realize that the Ladder of Stars exists in you; having discovered this, everything we study outside of ourselves - siderally - we learn exists within ourselves; we are the universe and our growth is in our planes of consciousness; we study the external that we may learn to know the internal; every existing power of the universe is in us.

****

Lecture # 17

THE BEMBINE TABLE OF ISIS

Manly P. Hall   6/15/1928

Unpublished Pages of "*The Secret Teachings of All Ages*"

LECTURES BY MANLY P. HALL   NO. 17
                                                                    6/15/28

THE BEMBINE TABLE OF ISIS

The three worlds are represented by the three main divisions of the Table; the divine or spiritual world is in the center; the world of intellect is above, and the world of matter is below - following the symbolism we have already given. The spiritual ego, or incarnating ego, is the seated figure of Isis; below is a box containing an animal - the symbol of the false self; the animal spirit - which is located beneath the throne of the spiritual ego.

There is some dispute in the minds of the modern school as to whether or not the Bembine Table is of antiquity; the statements in favor of it are in the majority. It was undoubtedly the work of an initiate; and its symbolism is absolute, complete and perfect. (You will find that the table carries a number of Greek and English letters; also some numbers. You must realize these were not part of the original but are the keys used to describe the text).

You will notice that each of the figures have upon their heads certain symbolic headdresses. Some of them are duplicated; these are composed, for the most part, of feathers and horns - they are the feather of Truth (The Eagle Feather is the Indian's symbol of truth, bravery and also spiritual comprehension). In many cases there are evidences of religious sects being included; the figures below that marked X in the lower panel - a man with the head of a bird;- the figure next to the right is crowned with horns, and in between the horns is a star and circle; this is a Buddhist symbol. You will find emblems of a great many religions and philosophies summed up in this table.

In considering the central figure of Isis, you will see the sacred cat; powerful because of its magnetism (also it has the habit of rolling up in the form of a ball - the endless circle of eternity). If you will examine the throne you will see two little globes with wings - the Egyptian symbol of the Trinity; the Father God, the Son God and the Warrior God were symbolized by the wings, the globe and the circle. (See Page 49) Amen, the Father God (Unknown Supreme Deity); Ra - or Ray, the Son Life, or Power; Osiris, the Destroyer, the Egyptian Trinity - minus the serpents - is reproduced on the Throne of Isis in this Bembine Table. In ancient symbolism the spiritual nature of man is represented by the globe; in it we have the seed germ - the activity principles. These wings are made of 'Vril' - the unknown motive power - the secret power possessed by the Egyptians. These two little globes, above the arch of the canopy, are the Over-Soul - the Anthropos. Isis represents the Incarnating consciousness. The spiritual nature of man is presumed to have descended from the Eternal Flame of Being - the One Fire, the One Life and the One Power. (The little row of tongues of fire represent the Great Sea of Divine Fire, from which spirit has its origin).

So here we have the symbols of the conscious spiritual nature of man; if you will look on the head of Isis you see she wears the horns of the ram; here we have a new key - the process of the spirit taking on form and passing through the cycle of Necessity has its analogy in the zodiac. As the year begins when the Sun, by the progression of the equinoxes, rises over the horizon - so these symbols represent the beginning of incarnating life; the beginning of spiritual manifestation - in the sign of Aries, represented by the horns. The Eye (between the horns) is a crude Egyptian hieroglyph, representing the Third Eye, or pineal gland, which has its seat in Aries, the Head. Isis is therefore represented as the Incarnating Spirit, enthroned in Aries. The Sun, in Aries, is powerful because it is the beginning of the new life of the year; when the sun enters Aries seedlings begin to sprout; life begins to flow; thus the Givers of Life are shown with horns to represent their ability to give life to man.

Isis is shown as a feminine symbol because out of it comes manifestation; it is the Matrix, or container of form; its progeny issue from the Great Mother. (It is also symbolized as the Father Power; in India both a god and goddess). This whole structure of the center throne room, in the nature of man, is the heart; on each side you find a triad - these figures represent the six vital organs which - with the Son, in the center of the head, are contained within the main part of the human body and are the most sacred and secret parts of man (analogous to the planets).

The two triads (on the right and left) give us seven figures (with Isis); these are called the double letters of the Hebrew alphabet. The Hebrew alphabet consists of 22 characters; these are divided into three sections - one containing three letters called the Mother letters; a second section consists of seven letters; called the double letters; and the third section of twelve, called the simple letters. According to philosophy the 21 powers or potencies come out of the Sun; therefore the number of the Sun is 21 in Pythagorean numerology.

(See Tarot Cards; page CXXIX) You will see 21 cards grouped on the 22nd. The Tarot consists of two divisions; you will note that the unnumbered card has been enlarged until it is made the size of the whole page, and the other 21 cards are laid on it. he numberless card is called the Fool in Tarot symbolism; according to the best work we have found, it is a cunningly concealed use of a very early Platonic axiom: 'It takes the wisest man in all the world to be the fool'. The Fool is the symbol of the Absolute itself - a daring symbol. It is the No-Thing. Thing means form; the Absolute has no parts, it has no element of matter in its nature; and in being No-Thing, it is well symbolized by the Fool. (The Sun represents the concentrated and unified nature; out of this numberless agency we draw the 21 numbered emanations). The unity of the Absolute is broken up into infinite diversity; the parts of the Divine symbolized by the cards; when properly re-established they become emblematic of the agencies of life, all of which are included in the Sum of Being. All the other cards are simply the zero card, broken up to form a deck. The 21 emblematic of three triads of 7's, coming out of the Absolute.

(Page 119) This diagram represents a cross section of Creation according to the Kabala. (Designed by Mr. Hall). Ain Soph is The Boundless, occupies the space of three rings - it breaks the two at the top. (If all the rings within the outer circle are removed you have a zero; everything from that outer circle to the center represents continual limitations of that one Substance). You will find the circles marked XI - XII and XIII as follows:

XI	XII	XIII
AIN	AIN SOPH	AIN SOPH AUR
(10th Sphere)	(9th Sphere)	(8th Sphere)
(Fiery Water; the Universe is formed by the process of concentration inward).	(The state of Universal Being)	(The Eternal Light)

Inside you will find four sets of ten rings; A-1 to A-10; B-1 to B-10, etc. The 4 worlds of the Kabala (of 10 rings) (See the Grand Man of the Zohar) Head is in the Absolute (Worlds A-1: A-10) his breast in Briah (B-1 to B-10); the generative system in Yetzirah (Worlds C-1 to C-10) and his feet on the earth and water (D-1 to D-10); there are the worlds of illusion or limitation - illusion of existence.

Creation is the process of creating these rings downward, slowly. The first ring is more important than the second; the second more important than the third; etc. This is because the further they go towards the center they become more material - the more spiritual towards the circumference.

(See page 123). The 10 globes connected by 22 paths (22 letters of the Hebrew alphabet) here we have the same diagram as in the Bembine Table (Translated from the Latin)

    (Above) the Horizon of Eternity - Ain Soph
           Symbol of the Anthropos

(1) Contains 10 words; in the center, Kether, the Crown. This is the beginning of spiritual man; the First Person of the Creative Triad.
(2) Chocma - Wisdom: the Second Person of the First triad of powers.
(3) Binah - Intelligence, the Third Person.

(1, 2 and 3 represent the Trinity of Spiritual Powers)
Kether, the Supreme Crown is the Eternal One; the Ancient of Ancients; the Macroprosophus; see one page back) the Tree of Life; you will find the tree growing out of the Crown, inverted; its roots in Eternity, its branches in Time.

On the right the Great Mother and Great Father (Chochma and Binah) These give birth to the Son (towards the center of the plate) - a circle called the Tiphereth - the Son - the beginning of the generations.

(4:
5-6-7-8
and 9) Around the Son you will find five other groups; in the form of a "U" two on each side and 1 below; these 6, plus Binah, are the Seven, the Elohim or spirits of creation.

(10) The 10th group, at the bottom, is called, in the Kabala, the Bride if the Microprosophus; the Lesser Face (The Lesser Adam). Its branches reaching down into matter.

                      ****

(See Page 185: Dante) You will see why Dante has received the honor of being included among the adepts.

At the center of the golden triangle at the top you find the Rose; each one of the petals represents one of the hierarchies. (The problem of life and death has come up in a question, which we will discuss by means of this plate).

You will find each one of the blue rings is connected by a thread to the circle above - which is the Archetype, from which all form comes; (the rings of which are the potentialities; the blue rings represent the potencies). That which is above represents the creative sphere - the dwelling place of Light; that which is below represents the spheres of existence or manifestation. The bank containing the stars - these are the fixed stars or zodiac - within this is the system of the universe (Ptolemy)

Incarnation is the process of descending from the sphere of the fixed stars down the rungs of the ladder to the globe in the center. This globe is divided into several parts; the blue is the ocean; the brown the earth; in the earth part there is a red triangle going into the earth; this represents the Inferno. A thread connects this triangle with the pyramid on the water; this pyramid is the ancient symbol of Paradise - the Terrestrial Heaven. On the top is a little cross of red; here, in his ascension, to reality - Dante met Beatrice, after he had been released from the services of Virgil.

The white sphere surrounding the earth represents the elements; according to the Egyptians, incarnation of man was downward through these rings, until at physical birth he occupied the position of the earth; he then passes through the three conditions of earth; having mastered these tests, then by the 7-runged ladder of Mithras he climbs up through the seven worlds until he reaches liberation.

A recapitulation of the processes within the nature of man itself; his auric nature consists of seven bodies (shown as the 7 planets). The group, including earth, has four elements - the etheric double, or vital body - the Linga Sharira - is the Moon. On upward through the other bodies in order, until we reach the Sun, which is Mind. We then continue upward until we come to the sphere of the fixed stars; when we reach this point we have mastered the various elements of our own bodies; then we ascend to the white circle, which is the spiritual realm, Nirvana - the place of liberation, from the Wheel of the Law. (Eight spokes, representing 8 limitations of being; finally annihilated in the 9th sphere, - the 10th being the Causal Sphere).

)))))))))))))

Lecture # 18

ON USE OF THE BOOK – BIBLIOGRAPHY AND INDEX

Manly P. Hall   6/16/1928

Unpublished Pages of "*The Secret Teachings of All Ages*"

LECTURES BY MANLY P. HALL   NO. 18
                                                               6/16/28

ON THE USE OF THE BOOK

(BIBLIOGRAPHY - AND THE INDEX)

SUGGESTED READING:

ADAMS Marsham	THE HOUSE OF THE HIDDEN PLACES	(Very valuable; one of the best works in existence on the mysticism of the Great Pyramid) Sometimes found in Public Libraries.
AGRIPPA	THREE BOOKS OF OCCULT PHILOSOPHY OR MAGIC	(Extremely scarce; the 2nd Vol of no value; the first part <u>is</u> of value)
ANONYMOUS:	THE CANON MANKIND: THEIR ORIGIN & DESTINY	(Both valuable, and rare; the 2nd may be found 'second-hand')
BABBITT, EDWIN D	PRINCIPLES OF LIGHT & COLOR	(Only authentic work available)
BACON, FRANCIS	NOVUM ORGANUM	
CUMONT, FRANZ	MYSTERIES OF MITHRA	
DOYLE	NATURE SPIRITS	
DUNLAP, S F	THE MYSTERIES OF ADONI	(Used by HPB in the Secret Doctrine)
FERGUSSON	TREE AND SERPENT WORSHIP	(Found in some libraries)
FRAZER, SIR JAMES	THE GOLDEN BOUGH	(Very valuable)
HAMILTON, SIR WM	METAPHYSICS AND LOGIC	(Standard text book)
HARTMAN, FRANZ		(All valuable, if obtainable)
HECKETHORNE	SECRET SOCIETIES OF ALL AGES	(Standard work)
HEINDEL MAX	ROSICRUCIAN PHILOSOPHY	
HIGGINS, GODFREY	ANACALYPSIS	(One book that stands alone; 200 copies of which 100 were burned; 100 copies of 1st Edition in existence; represents 30 yr's work; one of the great books of last century; author died before its completion)
KALISCH ISIDOR	THE SEPHER YEZIRAH	(Translation from Hebrew: the best)
KILNER, WALTER	THE HUMAN ATMOSPHERE	(The first man to reveal to the scientific world the auric bodies of man)
KINGSBOROUGH	ANTIQUITIES OF MEXICO	(Only copy in Los Angeles Library given to the City)
LEVI, ELIPHAS	TRANSCENDENTAL MAGIC	(Only book in which Levi gives his philosophy; his other writings are an effort to cover it up)
MEAD, G R S	APPOLONIUS OF TYANA THRICE GREAT HERMES	
MUIR, SIR WM	LIFE OF MOHAMMED	
MEYER, ISAAC	QUABBALAH	

OAKLEY I COOPER	COMTE DE ST GERMAINE	(Very fine; very rare)
O'NEILL JOHN	NIGHT OF THE GODS	
ROSENROTH KORR		(Most important work on the Kabala ever written; the only copy west of the Mississippi in the Sutro Collection in Special room in San Fran Library)
SKINNER	THE SOURCES OF MEASURES	(HPB quotes liberally from this work in the Secret Doctrine)
SMYTHE, CHAS P	OUR INHERITANCE IN THE GREAT PYRAMID	
STANLEY	HISTORY OF PHILOSOPHY	(One of 4 books that is important on life of Pythagoras)
TAYLOR THOS	DISSERTATION ON THE ELUSINIAN MYSTERIES	(Nearly all his works are rare)
	IAMBLICHUS ON THE MYSTERIES	(Very rare; Taylor is the greatest Platonist of the modern world)
WAITE A W	THE SECRET DOCTRINE IN ISRAEL	(Best work)
WESTCOTT WM		(One of the few things in English on Bembine Table of Isis)
WILSON	VISHNU PURANA	(Used by HPB in the Secret D.)

******

The Index may be used separately from the book itself, as a dictionary; or as a guide to the book. Each line contains the essence of the treatment - boiled down carefully. There are, in reality, three books in one; the text - the plates, and the captions under the plates. They are related necessarily to each other - but they form three complete books).

As an example: "LUCIFER" - the Index shows four references (CCXXIX) You will find considerable material in the four references to meditate upon.

(1) Page 148 (CXLVIII) This particular work is a scarce item and will bring much material to your attention previously unpublished. Lucifer is the greatest mystery of symbolism.
Table 13 - Figure 1 is Ain.Soph; Fig II - the Three Divine Principles θ Father, Son and Holy Ghost; the Dot is Lucifer; it represents the Fire of Heaven; the fall of that fire into the material fire; Lucifer means the Light Bearer - the Fire of God. (This diagram is an important one) See two diagrams on preceding pages; also important. Page 146 - these are the plan of the Tomb of C R C (Nos 4 & 5) C R C represents a cosmic principle; the Tomb is the universe (the tomb was made as a miniature of the universe)

(2) Page 68: See diagram of the tetractys - the most sacred of Pythagorean figures; It is a golden symbol, and its meaning is legion; the sum of knowledge is enclosed in this triangle and many things can be gained by an understanding of it. Musical ratios of the ancients; it represents the 10 numbers; The One of the Monad becomes the Two - the Duad or Illusionary Universe (Mind). From From the Two comes the Three (Soul) - the 3 primary parts of the universe; below the Four (Body) secondary parts or lower universe.
It is 'Atlantis'; the seed world from which the generations come. This Pyramid of Dots is one of the supreme symbols of ancient philosophy. The Pythagoreans believed that by meditation on this symbol they would come into all wisdom.

(3) Page 51: We know that the Sun is the symbol of power; here we have the 3 Suns; the Spiritual Sun (Vulcan) the Soular Sun (Christ) and the Material Sun (Lucifer) Lucifer is the material mind - the thing that leads man to the accumulation of material knowledge; it is the illusion of worldliness. According to philosophy the spiritual nature of man, or man as Being, was individualized in the mind substance; therefore man is peculiarly a mental creature, and Lucifer is the

symbol of Man in the sense of Manas, or the Thinker. In the highest phases of philosophy there comes the realization that the mind is the supreme snarer of consciousness; and in some of the ancient mysteries the mind was symbolized by a net. The net of thinking - the mind of man is the enemy of consciousness, and yet is a necessary implement, for the time, at least. It is the thing that lures consciousness out of its own realization into the acceptance and involvement of popular thought; it is the mind that has urged the building of a great physical empire - this earth; to maintain a great Juggernaut, and we throw ourselves under the wheels at eternal sacrifices. Mind is continually involving; the mind that rules the life was symbolized by Lucifer.

******

(You will find these things have a great deal to do with philosophy. Gold represents the spiritual consciousness; the base metals, the material consciousness, which must be continually refined and purified and elevated).

The word 'Christ' is a title; signifying One in Whom the great work has been accomplished; the 'great work' is the transmutation of the base metal or base nature into the spiritual nature; base metal represents diversity; and the return of diversity to Unity is the development. The royal road to attainment is signified as a path upward through diversity to Unity. The state of consciousness attained is dignified by a peculiar term; the state of realization has its own name or term, and he who attains this state of realization - this grasp - takes upon himself the name of the state or condition he attains. 'The Christ' represents universal consciousness, and he who is 'Christened' has attained the state of universal consciousness; He becomes The Christ; the state is ONE, and the consciousness of the individual is absorbed into the superior consciousness, and, to a certain degree, these higher Names incarnate in those who attain. It is a condition of supreme realization, and any who come to this condition of spiritual Knowing, Understanding is signified by the term 'Christ'.

Lucifer represents Intellectualism; there is but one Lucifer; but any one who is ambitious to attain the heights of worldliness - is Lucifer.

****

Plato has said the mind is a part of the Illusion - but the one part capable of knowing the reality; it is by the mind that we learn to know there is something higher than the mind. The mind is the thing by which we judge the mind; it is incapable of reality, but it shows us reality. By the intellect man learns to know there is Truth; Truth is above Mind and the mind can never think what Truth IS; it knows its existence abstractly; it is the bridge across which man must pass from unconsciousness to consciousness. It knows it must die, that the greater may live; the mind makes the supreme sacrifice in order that consciousness may go on (this is the deepest fact we can reveal). Man fights against his lower mind; finally reaches the higher mind, and then the higher mind says 'there is something I cannot grasp'. By the higher mind philosophic truths are revealed, and man, in realizing them, leaves the mind behind; he casts off thought as he casts off bodies.

Philosophy has as its purpose the development of something that is not philosophy but something that transcends philosophy; their art is to stimulate a super-mental power (this faculty only works occasionally, leaving a flash of understanding that comes almost like a mental light; it illuminates, and then goes out). The purpose of philosophy is to awaken this faculty of understanding naturally - by building so carefully and so firmly that the mind gradually rises to the grasping of higher things and ultimately surpassing itself. It is a faculty of knowing without thinking; it jumps over the processes of mental activity and is still knowing; it is a higher faculty but one must first pass through the mental processes; this super mental process is a gradual unfoldment; claircognizance is far above the limitation of mind.

Lecture # 19

SYMBOLISM

Manly P. Hall   6/17/1928

Unpublished Pages of "*The Secret Teachings of All Ages*"

LECTURES BY MANLY P. HALL   NO. 19

SYMBOLISM

The purpose of our work this evening is to consider the purpose of symbolism as a part of philosophy. Symbolism is a very important element in the education of the human mind. You know children are almost always educated first with the aid of pictures; the picture precedes the word and the letter, and pictures, unlike words, know no language; a picture means the same thing to any race, and whether an individual understands your language or not he can understand the picture. The great truths of life are expressed by means of symbolic pictures, and symbolism is a language more ancient, more universal, more powerful, than any other language in the world.

In philosophy the symbol is more important than any written description; most of the elements with which philosophy is concerned cannot be pictured; an effort to picture them limits them, and the symbol is far more appropriate than a word. It appeals to a sense perception more acute than the ear - more quick to respond -- the eye. The eye is peculiarly powerful - particularly close to understanding. By means of the eye we are able to instruct people with the aid of the symbol quicker than by the use of the printed page. Symbolic philosophy, we feel, has a very important place in the world today.

For nearly a century the greatest minds of the world have been concentrating on the most important issue of the world - world peace. Gradually we are realizing that war is not only a survival of barbarism, but it is the least productive. Now there are several awards offered annually to those who will suggest the most appropriate methods of outlawing war. We feel that war is simply one of the many effects that have as their common cause a lack of understanding. War is the result of the fact that man has never learned to understand man; various races and nations are laboring under a deluded form of patriotism that overlooks brotherhood.

Before we can hope to bring people together we must increase the number of things people have in common. Our friendships are based on the things we have in common. Our animosities are based on the things one person has and another person wants; the things we understand together we are agreed upon; the things we do not understand together we are disagreed upon, and disagreement is the first step to war. Ignorance is now simply ig - norance; it is wilfully overlooking the things we should understand.

We have several causes of war; probably the two greatest are defined by Plato; the first is the necessity for increasing land possessions; races outgrow the borders of their own states and find it necessary to increase the land area they occupy. The second cause of war in history has been the religious element; wherever it is found that people have narrow religious viewpoints it is also noticeable there is continual friction among them. There is a third cause for war, that was not recognized in Plato's time - wars are financially successful - they have a profound effect on the financial condition of the world. The ulterior motive of gain enters in the situation.

In symbolism, it seems to me, we have a very important method of reaching people. Today we are divided, by language, by racial customs, by attitudes, by ideals - from the other nations of the earth. Each people has its own hopes, aspirations; but in the lack of this understanding - of that which is the ideal of all living - we have the basis of our great sociological and political unrest. As soon as we understand the meaning of life - really - we will begin to live in accordance with that understanding.

We have come to the agreement that that is best which is the greatest good to the greatest number; that which serves the majority is conceived to be the greatest good. Consequently - while we may not be able to know at this time the absolute nature of good - relative good is that which today serves most completely the needs of the greatest number. Now, we have tried in several ways to create or invent some method of bringing people closer together; two efforts were made by language - to create an international language. (Esperanto).

In philosophy we have also the possibilities of world language; in fact we have a world language now and do not know it; that is the language of symbols. Symbolism has been used since the beginning of time as a method of perpetuating ideals. We are living in a very real world; yet we will never be able to solve the problem of our race until we become involved in the more profound purpose of philosophy; it is to show us how to exist <u>together</u>. Science can teach us how to exist; but it requires more than science to <u>exist</u> together. Philosophy is concerned with man's relation to man; trying to improve the conditions of one person to another - the spreading of understanding of those higher issues that help to bring life <u>together</u>.

We have been talking to you about philosophy for many evenings; we want to try to talk to you about the use of philosophy - what philosophy means to the world; how it has been applied to the solution of the problems of the world. Never has history recorded a people controlled by philosophy. If such a condition could have existed we believe a reasonably perfect environment would have resulted. We find the philosopher has a peculiar advantage; a great philosopher has, first of all, convinced himself; therefore he has converted the hardest person first - and it is a great thing to convert one's self. Philosophy adds a power inside; philosophy even discovers - according to its own ideas - a strength in Self, and that strength in Self, which it postulates, makes the philosopher and his strength greater than all the rest of the universe together. The strength in the absolute belief in reality and the truth of philosophy makes the philosopher master of the world. Philosophy brings fraternity; it changes the standards of value - lifting thought above matter; it declares that he who is strong in mind is stronger than he who is strong in body. It also shows that from the beginning of time, and to the end of time, mind will rule matter. Philosophy postulates something absolutely necessary; viz: that it is not sufficient to have a mind. It is necessary to have a mind in which certain qualities are manifesting. In order to have a mind sane and capable of being of value to other minds it must have certain qualities in itself; it must have integrity. Integrity is a quality of thinking; it is an element in life - invisible but all-powerful.

The human mind passes through three stages; the first of which is theology; the second metaphysics, and the third, positivism. (Positivism is almost synonomous with modern science). If you will look at the picture of the human life you will find it divided into three great epochs; in periods of growth, maturity and decay. Birth opens the effort to growth; maturity represents the most complete physical power; and in advanced age we find the third division, in the ancient system of thinking. The first period is given over to learning; the second to labor, and the third to reflection. (It is presumed that life is a gradual mental growth).

True philosophy represents the very highest expression of human knowledge. There is no branch that goes any higher than philosophy. But philosophy, unlike science, is working with an element much less concrete than science. Science, moving cautiously, is able, to a degree, to prove its findings; it requires a more highly organized mind to have a thing proved mentally than it does to have it proved physically. Science has one advantage over philosophy; it can show the object it is studying; philosophy cannot - it must convert through reason, whereas science converts through the eye. As the mind is higher than the eye, it requires a more highly evolved intelligence to see the working of mental processes than it does to see the workings of physical processes. Philosophy has never descended to the level of phenomena.

Philosophy assures man that the answer to the heartache is only comprehensible to the rational thinker; consequently it does not get out and try to convert the world - because to convert the world you must give it what it understands. Philosophy knows that the mind that is ignorant wants miracles; philosophy is limited to people who think. Philosophy cannot work with people who have completely closed systems of thinking from which they cannot be moved. It can only work with the mind that is beginning to grasp its own ignorance, and at the same time unfolding certain rational faculties in itself. When the mind reaches a certain degree of thinking certain things become apparent, and until they become apparent there is no way of making them apparent. Once this begins to unfold, then the mind begins reaching out to philosophy; this mass begins to organize; the individual who has evolved these rational faculties begins to see why Plato said what he said and how Plato knew he was right. Not until the mind rises out of the ruts of theology, until it begins the grasp of an inner working - to study the phenomena of his own being and begins to organize a vast amount of material - does he suddenly begin to understand the workings of philosophy.

Philosophy has a very simple program to offer mankind; it says there are certain realities; you can assume these things are so because they are necessary (and necessary because they are so). Philosophy declares that certain things are good; Socrates declared that certain words were synonomous with good; that virtue and good and utility were synonomous. The philosophers of all ages have declared that Beauty is a fundamental cosmic reality ; it is natural for things to be beautiful - philosophy moves on that assumption. It further declares that which is beautiful is good, and that which is beautiful and good has the greatest utilitarian value. Philosophy presumes that that which is beautiful is practical, for Beauty is the symmetry of parts; in Beauty there is harmony, and harmony is the harmonious adjustment of parts.

There are two kinds of truths; truths considered to be absolute and basic, and truths considered secondary and relative. (Existing conditions - consequently true, while the conditions remain). Philosophy offers a solution, with special privileges to none and equal opportunities to all. It brings the problem back to natural order, declaring that the laws of the universe and man are suitable for governing the state; the laws that govern human affairs should be the laws that govern the universal affairs.

Where there is philosophy in the life there cannot be selfishness in the life. We cannot be hurt unless we give the weapon which hurts into the hand of our adversary. All over the world there are people grieving - hungry - sick - sorrowful - as well as in physical pain; the various branches of philosophy, including science and religion, have the solutions to the majority of these problems.

****

Lecture # 20

CONSCIOUSNESS HOW TO READ THE 'SECRET TEACHINGS' BOOK

Manly P. Hall   6/18/1928

Unpublished Pages of "*The Secret Teachings of All Ages*"

LECTURES BY MANLY P. HALL

NO. 20
6/18/28

(a) CONSCIOUSNESS
    (State of Knowing)

(c) MENTAL LEVEL
    (Vanishing Point)

(b) MATERIALISM
    (Tracing everything to
    Form as Base)

(Energy superior to Matter;
Manifesting thru multiplicity
of Forms)

The vanishing point (c) of matter is where Form becomes so infinitely minute there is no substance known to physical power capable of holding it, or even estimating it. It is the mental level - the line between noumena (power of the Knower) and phenomena (the thing to be known). One ascends from the least degree of matter to the least degree of spiritual awareness.

******

(CONCERNING THE BOOK)

We are going to imagine that you are in your own home with the Book and you want to know how to study it. I want to briefly give you the first suggestions. If you have taken notes of these lectures you will later realize something important; while these have not been quoting from page after page of the book, they are concerned with the substance of the book. It is a book of symbols; and instead of being a book directly on symbols, we have made it a philosophy of symbols. The book is as nearly in order as we can arrange it.

Begin at the beginning; begin with the Introduction. Read it through very carefully and not only read it through, in the ordinary sense, but think about it. Read one paragraph at a time. No More. Do not read a page and then think about it; you will have too many confusing ideas at once. When you have read the paragraph and have committed to your mind the distinguishing element or feature involved - take that element, apply it to the things around you; try to see the working of the thing you have read; think about it; work with it; apply it and see if you can make it fit into some condition of actual life. Take the subject, apply it to your philosophy; your religion, your morals, etc., and work out the correspondences until you come to know all the ramifications of the paragraph. Do this conscientiously. If your first reasonings are consistent you will build up the system upon which it is all worked. You will then have a reasonably brief, but complete, basis upon which to estimate the thinking of the world. You will learn classification of thought. In the Introduction we have given a brief summary of the great keynotes of the great thinkers, and by familiarizing yourself with them you will note what the world has thought for the last 2600 years. Also, you will undoubtedly find something else: that your own mind will be particularly attracted to one or two sects or groups; that certain of these schools agree with your thinking - certain of these schools interest you more than others; they are closer to your thinking. With this as a tool you can develop it by reading the standard works of the particular philosopher. Do not ask questions; answer them.

Do not rest until you can explain things yourself. If you run across something involved and you cannot work it out, set yourself to that task, and work it out if it takes ten years; then you <u>know</u> something. This work is intended to be thought about every day; the book is intended to communicate to you the standards of ethics of these particular subjects.

Turn to Page 21: attack this the same way; on Page 22 there is a sub-title (Druidic) - on Page 23 (Right of Mithras). You see headings; instead of reading a paragraph - read all the material between one set of headings the first day. Get from that the picture; then the next day take the first paragraph; finally, analyze the material.

These paragraphs contain a variety of subject-matter; some paragraphs are purely historical (these stimulate a different set of faculties). Take your dictionary - your encyclopedia - anything from which you can find more about the subject matter; try to add to the matter treated. Work in this way right through the book.

Try to remember whether any paragraph you have previously read has anything to do with the subject on hand; go back, look it up and try to relate it. If you have made your relationship, back and forth, you will have woven it all into one fabric. If you do so, it will really mean something to you.

****

Acknowledgements and Recommendations

Thank you to all who made the publishing of this unprecedented manuscript possible:

Manly P. Hall – His wisdom and dedication to the Spirit of Truth.
Gary Koz Mraz – Creative Director, spiritualsedonamag@gmail.com.
Christiana Fior – Copy Editor, www.christinafior.com.
Ramsey Lucas – Graphic Artist.
Deborah L. Cambio – To my wife for her love and support.

Creative Director's Commentary

In the consolidation and design of this publication I was struck by Mr. Hall's sentence, "This book is like unto a door – a gate, in some old sanctuary, containing within it a wealth of imagery; a wealth of mysteries, designs and figures."

Having purchased my personal copy of The Secret Teachings of All Ages at the Manly P. Hall Library in Los Feliz, CA in 1975, I had looked at the cover hundreds of times, pondering its monumental subtitle: "Masonic Hermetic Cabalistic & Rosicrucian Symbolical Philosophy by Manly P. Hall." Was Mr. Hall's small rectangular title in the upper right corner his "door"? Was the empty space his sanctuary?

Is it possible something so symbolically obvious had gone unseen for so long? We may never know, but it unequivocally inspired the cover of this manuscript." Gary Koz Mraz - Creative Director

Editor's Recommendations

Recommendation: Although there are several companies publishing the "Secret Teachings of All Ages," I recommend that you purchase the original book published through Manly P. Hall's organization, The Philosophical Research Society, **www.prs.org**.

For comprehensive integrative health information on more than 300 health conditions go to: World Research Foundation www.wrf.org

Steven A. Ross
Editor, The Unpublished Pages of The Secret Teaching of All Ages
dearorpheus@gmail.com

Other Books by Steven A. Ross available at Amazon.
And Nothing Happened...But You Can Make It Happen.
A Grand Design of Dreams.

Less Complicated, Inc.
PO BOX 20756
Sedona, AZ 86341
www.lesscomplicated.net

www.ingramcontent.com/pod-product-compliance
Lightning Source LLC
Chambersburg PA
CBHW081200230426
43666CB00016B/2878